AN ADVOCATE'S [GUIDE]
TO COMPLAIN[TS]
IN ENGLAND

FOR PROFESSIONAL AND VOLUNTARY ADVOCATES SUPPORTING ADULTS, YOUNG PEOPLE AND CHILDREN THROUGH COMPLAINTS PROCEDURES

BY MUNA ADAM, LYNN BRADY AND MALCOLM JOHNSON

ILLUSTRATIONS BY GEORGINA WESTON

An Advocate's Guide To Complaints In England

© Muna Adam, Lynn Brady and Malcolm Johnson, 2018

The authors have asserted their rights in accordance with the Copyright, Designs and Patents Act (1988) to be identified as the authors of this work.

Published by:
Pavilion Publishing and Media Ltd
Rayford House
School Road
Hove
East Sussex
BN3 5HX
Tel: 01273 434 943
Fax: 01273 227 308
Email: info@pavpub.com

Published 2018

All rights reserved. No part of this publication may be reproduced, stored in a retrieval system, or transmitted in any form or by any means, electronic, mechanical, photocopying, recording or otherwise, without prior permission in writing of the publisher and the copyright owners.

A catalogue record for this book is available from the British Library.

ISBN: 978-1-911028-89-5

Pavilion is the leading training and development provider and publisher in the health, social care and allied fields, providing a range of innovative training solutions underpinned by sound research and professional values. We aim to put our customers first, through excellent customer service and value.

Cover image and all illustrations by Georgina Weston.

Authors: Muna Adam, Lynn Brady and Malcolm Johnson
Production editor: Ruth Chalmers, Pavilion Publishing and Media
Page layout and typesetting: Phil Morash, Pavilion Publishing and Media
Printing: CMP Digital Print Solutions

Contents

About the authors 7
Acknowledgements 8
Preface 10
Chapter 1: The role of the advocate 13
    1.1: The role of the advocate – overview 13
    1.2: Types of advocacy 14
    1.3: Non-instructed advocacy 16
    1.4: Alternative/augmented communication methods 17
    1.5: Advocacy training and qualifications 17
    1.6: Knowledge, skills and attributes needed for the advocacy role 18
    1.7: Access to advocacy 21
    1.8: National standards for advocacy organisations 22
    1.9: Policies and procedures for advocacy organisations 24
    1.10: The limits of the advocacy role 27
    1.11: Obtaining legal advice 28
    1.12: Key points 29
Chapter 2: The tasks of the advocate 31
    2.1: Overview 31
    2.2: The referral 31
    2.3: Planning the initial meeting 32
    2.4: The advocacy process 35
    2.5: Presenting a complaint 43
    2.6: Progressing the complaint 46
    2.7: Requesting records 51
    2.8: Understanding the complaint response 53
    2.9: Recognising the limits of the complaints procedure 54
    2.10: Key points 55
Chapter 3: Understanding the complaints system 57
    3.1: How are complaints systems set up? 57
    3.2: Different institutions working together 59
    3.3: Maladministration 60

3.4: How the complaints system works 61
3.5: The role of the Ombudsman and other similar institutions 61
3.6: The Local Government and Social Care Ombudsman (LGSCO) 62
3.7: The Draft Public Service Ombudsman Act 67
3.8: Other legal routes 68
3.9: Key points 73

Chapter 4: Complaints about children's services 75
4.1: Introduction 75
4.2: The complaints system for children's services 75
4.3: The duty to appoint an advocate 77
4.5: Voluntary organisations 84
4.6: Children's homes 84
4.7: Independent fostering agencies – The Fostering Services (England) Regulations (2011) 85
4.8: The role of the Local Government and Social Care Ombudsman (LGSCO) 86
4.9: Key points 87
4.10: Case studies from the LGSCO 87

Chapter 5: Complaints about social care 97
5.1: Overview 97
5.2: The complaints system for social care 97
5.3: Independent advocacy under the Care Act (2014) 98
5.4: The Local Authority Social Services and National Health Service Complaints (England) Regulations (2009) 99
5.5: Varying policies between local authorities 104
5.6: Key points 106
5.7: Case studies from the Local Government and Social Care Ombudsman 107

Chapter 6: Complaints about health services 119
6.1: The Care Quality Commission 119
6.2: The constitution and values of the NHS 120
6.3: The structure of the NHS 121
6.4: The statutory framework for the NHS complaints system 122
6.5: Independent advocacy and advice in the NHS 123
6.6: The Local Authority Social Services and National Health Service Complaints (England) Regulations (2009) 124

 6.7: The NHS Bodies and Local Authorities (Partnership Arrangements, Care Trusts, Public Health and Local Healthwatch) Regulations (2012) 127
 6.8: Making a complaint about a health service professional 128
 6.9: Private sector health service providers 131
 6.10: Mental Health 132
 6.11: The Parliamentary and Health Service Ombudsman (PHSO) 134
 6.12: Key points 136
 6.13: Case summaries 137

Chapter 7: Complaints about education 141
 7.1: Introduction 141
 7.2: The education structure in England 141
 7.3: State or maintained schools 143
 7.4: Complaints about independent schools 148
 7.5: Complaints about non-maintained special schools 149
 7.6: Complaints about higher education and universities 150
 7.7: Complaints about apprenticeships 151
 7.8: Key points 152

Chapter 8: Complaints about housing issues and planning 155
 8.1: The scheme for housing complaints 155
 8.2: Who can complain and what can they complain about? 156
 8.3: The role of the designated person 157
 8.4: Complaints about neighbour nuisance and antisocial behaviour 158
 8.5: The Housing Ombudsman 158
 8.6: The Homes and Communities Agency 159
 8.7: The Draft Public Service Ombudsman Bill 159
 8.8: Other housing issues that do not fall under The Housing Ombudsman's scheme 160
 8.9: Key points 160
 8.10: Case summaries 161

Chapter 9: Complaints about benefits 165
 9.1: Introduction 165
 9.2: Complaints and the appeals system for benefits 165
 9.3: How to submit a complaint – the procedure 166
 9.4: The role of the Parliamentary and Health Service Ombudsman 166
 9.5: Key points 167

Chapter 10: Complaints about the police and the crown prosecution service 169

    10.1: Introduction 169

    10.2: The Independent Office for Police Conduct (formerly the Independent Police Complaints Commission) 170

    10.3: The complaints system – an overview 171

    10.4: Complaints concerning discrimination 172

    10.5: Who can make a complaint? 172

    10.6: Who can be complained about? 173

    10.7: Time limits 173

    10.8: What can be complained about – conduct, 'direction and control' and death and serious injury (DSI) matters 174

    10.9: The initial procedure 175

    10.10: Discontinuance and suspending of a procedure 180

    10.11: The right of appeal 181

    10.12: Complaints about the Crown Prosecution Service 182

    10.13: The Code of Practice for Victims of Crime 182

    10.14: The CPS complaints procedure 184

    10.15: The Witness Charter 185

    10.16: The Victims' Right to Review Scheme 185

    10.17: The Child Sexual Abuse Review Panel 186

    10.18: The Victims' Commissioner 186

    10.19: Key points 186

Chapter 11: Complaints about utility and other private companies 189

    11.1: Introduction 189

    11.2: Utility services 189

    11.3: Procedures for complaining to utility companies 190

    11.4: Utility Ombudsmen and the water industry redress scheme 191

    11.5: Consumer complaints in other sectors 191

    11.6: Key points 194

Chapter 12: Complaints about data protection 197

    12.1: Introduction 197

    12.2: The Information Commissioner 197

    12.3: The Data Protection Act (1998) – data, processing, controllers and subjects 198

12.4: The data protection principles 198
12.5: What are people's rights under the Data Protection Act (1998)? 200
12.6: What can people do if their rights under the Data Protection Act are breached? 202
12.7: The Freedom of Information Act (2000) 204
12.8 The General Data Protection Regulation 205
12.9: Key points 205

Chapter 13: Complaints about lawyers 207
13.1: Introduction 207
13.2: Instructing a solicitor 208
13.3: The Law Society and the Solicitors Regulation Authority (SRA) 209
13.4: The Solicitors Regulation Authority's code of conduct 210
13.5: The ten principles of the code of conduct 210
13.6: Making a complaint against a solicitors firm 211
13.7: Professional errors made by solicitors and conflicts of interest 213
13.8: The Legal Ombudsman 214
13.9: Key points 215

Chapter 14: Complaints about the prison and probation service 217
14.1: Introduction 217
14.2: Different types of prisons 217
14.3: Probation 218
14.4: Her Majesty's Prison and Probation Service (HMPPS) 218
14.5: The complaints system for prisoners 218
14.6: Probation Instructions 51/2014 – the complaints system for people on probation 220
14.7: The Prisons and Probation Ombudsman (PPO) 221
14.8: Key points 222

Index of statutes and statutory instruments 225
Subject index 231

About the authors

Malcolm Johnson

Malcolm is a Solicitor at Hudgells, where he specialises in personal injury and clinical negligence claims. He is a Solicitor Advocate, a member of the Law Society's Personal Injury Panel, and a Fellow of the Association of Personal Injury Lawyers.

Malcolm is an Adviser to Coram Voice, where he assists their advocates in making complaints on behalf of looked after-children and care leavers.

Dr Lynn Brady

Lynn is an Advocate and an Independent Person for Children Act complaints. She has a PhD in social care specialising in the needs of traumatised young people in the care system, who have challenging behaviour. She also has a postgraduate teaching qualification as well as professional qualifications in advocacy for children and young people, childcare, counselling, NVQ assessment and verification. For the past 40 years all of her work has been linked to improving the lives of children, young people and families – particularly those who are disadvantaged and/or disengaged either in the community, education or training.

Muna Adam

Muna has worked and volunteered with vulnerable people, in the UK and abroad, for over ten years. She is an experienced Youth Advocate with an extensive knowledge of children's rights and the care system. This work has also required her to have a broad understanding of housing, education, mental health and welfare systems.

Muna is working as a Senior Paralegal in a local authority and she is completing her Legal Practice Course.

Acknowledgements

The authors would like to thank the following for their kind help with this book.

Andri Ellina helped us by drafting the case studies in Chapters 4 and 5.

Patricia Wakeford – Senior Associate in the Clinical Negligence Department of BL Claims helped us with Chapter 6.

Renu Daly – Senior Solicitor in the Clinical Negligence Department at Hudgells helped us with Chapter 6.

Guy Micklewright – Barrister in the Professional Regulatory Department of Blake Morgan helped us with Chapter 6.

Laurie Avadis – Principal of Avadis & Co helped us with Chapters 3 and 4.

Gwen James
7th November 1929 – 21st September 2015

This book is dedicated to Gwen James, who founded Voice for the Child in Care. Throughout her life she campaigned for the right of children and young people in the care system to be able to make a complaint about their treatment. This led directly to the incorporation of this right in the 1989 Children Act. Complaints procedures are now a recognised and established policy throughout the social care field.

Preface

This book is concerned with complaints brought on behalf of both adults and children. It describes the different types of advocacy provided to complainants and the role and tasks of the advocate; it collates and explains the various sources of guidance for advocates (who present or assist with complaints); it describes the process of how a complaint is initially made; and follows through the various stages of complaints and advises on how best to achieve a positive outcome.

We have attempted to provide 'hands on' advice with a minimum of legal jargon. We hope that this book can be used as a handbook for all those who undertake this kind of work, either in a professional or voluntary capacity.

In the first three chapters, we have tried to describe the advocacy world, to explain how this fits with the legal system, and to answer the general questions commonly put by advocates who are dealing with difficult cases. At the end of each chapter, we have tried to provide a helpful 'Key points' section. In the subsequent chapters we go into detail about the respective complaints procedures of various organisations. Where possible we have included examples of cases that have progressed to higher bodies such as Ombudsmen or courts (as complaints themselves are not made public). We hope thereby to give examples of the type of complaints that are successful.

It is envisaged that the advocate should be able to dip into these subsequent chapters for advice as and when needed. Although several institutions have published summaries and other brief pieces of information about different respective complaints processes, we have tried to provide a comprehensive route map for the main complaints systems that we have in England. This should be particularly helpful for advocates dealing with complaints that may cross between different institutions, such as social care and mental health. In some chapters, the summary that we have provided is relatively brief but it is designed to give the advocate a rough idea of how the system works and where to look for guidance.

The scope of this book does not cover all institutions but only those institutions which the writers felt impacted mostly on their clients. For example, we have not covered the complaints system operated by the Home Office in relation to immigration (for which expert advice should be sought) or the Financial Services Authority.

A word of advice to readers

Contact details for advocacy providers have not been included in this book. This is because independent advocacy services are commissioned locally by organisations such as local authorities and the NHS to provide advocacy services for their clients. In practice, this means that advocacy providers are likely to change when contracts expire. Therefore it is always important to make contact with the organisation to find out who their current advocacy provider is and also to check the advocacy services available to clients.

A word of advice to advocates

This book was written as a guide for advocates. It cannot be used as a substitute for legal advice or up-to-date research in any one case. The law changes rapidly and guide books fall behind. Advocates always need to check that their information is up-to-date. There are also situations where advocates need to recognise the limits of their competence and to know when to refer a client to a suitably qualified lawyer. Below we set out a legal disclaimer.

Disclaimer

This book is produced for the assistance of advocates submitting complaints to local authorities and other organisations. It is not intended to stand as legal advice in any particular case, and should not be relied upon as such. To the extent permitted by law, the authors will not be liable by reason of breach of contract, negligence, or otherwise for any loss or consequential loss occasioned to any person acting, omitting to act or refraining from acting in reliance upon the book or arising from or connected with any error or omission in the book. Consequential loss shall be deemed to include, but is not limited to, any loss of profits or anticipated profits, damage to reputation, or goodwill, loss of business or anticipated business, damages, costs, expenses incurred or payable to any third party or any other indirect or consequential losses.

HOW TO BE A SUPER ADVOCATE
ADVOCATE TRAINING
BE...
PROFESSIONAL
HONEST
OPEN MINDED
KNOWLEDGABLE
APPROACHABLE
FRIENDLY
GOOD AT LISTENING
EXPERIENCED
EMPATHETIC
REASSURING
HARD WORKING
MAKE A DIFFERENCE

Chapter 1: The role of the advocate

1.1: The role of the advocate – overview

The aim of this chapter is to explain the role of an advocate in a complaints process. This is not straightforward as the demands of the role may differ depending on the service being complained about and on the needs and abilities of the child, young person or adult who wishes to make the complaint.

The role of advocacy, in its broadest sense, is to support another person to make sure that their concerns, wishes and feelings are heard, that their rights are upheld and that service providers meet their needs. This support may or may not lead to a formal complaint.

Complaints help institutions improve their services by identifying where things have gone wrong or where things could be done in a different and/or better way. Although nobody likes to receive complaints, the majority of complaint handlers recognise the importance of complaints and are very supportive of clients who are pursuing a complaint. It is always in the institution's interests, as well as the clients', to resolve complaints at the earliest stage and as swiftly as is possible. The role of the advocate is to help to ensure that clients make clear, manageable complaints and that clients understand the process. Most complaints handlers welcome support from advocates and are happy to cooperate and liaise with advocacy services, recognising the benefits they bring to the complaints process and the quality of services provided to their clients.

Professional and voluntary advocacy services have developed in recognition of the fact that vulnerable children and adults often experience difficulties in getting their voices heard about matters that affect them.

Professional and voluntary advocates should not be confused with 'legal advocates' who are solicitors and barristers.

The term to describe a user of advocacy services differs between agencies; some refer to the child or adult as a 'service user' others may refer to the 'client', or 'advocacy partner'. If the advocate is an informal volunteer providing advocacy support, the person carrying out the advocacy role may be a relative, friend or colleague. For the purposes of this book the person who receives advocacy support will be known as 'the client'.

The major difference between the role of an advocate and most other professionals is that it is not an advocate's role to decide what is in the client's best interests. Instead the aim is to make sure that the client's voice is heard, and listened to, when others are making 'best interest' decisions about them.

Although parts of the advocate's role may differ depending on the organisation's client group, the fundamental aim of advocacy is to listen, understand the reasons for the complaint and to know what outcomes the client wants.

Advocates are dealing with situations where public services have gone wrong. It is important to approach each case with an open mind and realise that there is a great deal of exemplary public service happening. The role of the complaints system is to help to improve those services.

1.2: Types of advocacy

There are different types of advocates who can support a client to submit a complaint. The advocate's job or role title is often related to the work they do with the client and where their work is carried out.

Advocates work in a range of settings. Some advocates work across several settings – they may be office-based, working in the community, visiting clients at home, or they may be based in statutory and/or voluntary institutions. Examples include: care homes, mental health hospitals, secure units, young offenders institutions, social care placements, and health or education provisions.

Types of advocacy	Description	Clients
Independent Mental Health Advocate (IMHA).	This type of advocate must hold the IMHA qualification.	Children, young people or vulnerable adults who have been, or are likely to be, detained under the Mental Health Act 1983.

Independent Mental Capacity Advocate (IMCA).	This type of advocate must hold the IMCA qualification.	Young people who are aged 16 or over and vulnerable adults who lack the capacity to make independent decisions under the Mental Capacity Act (2005).
Care Act Advocate (CAA).	This type of advocate must be qualified – see 1.5.	Adults who require care assessment, care and support planning, care and support reviews and safeguarding under the Care Act (2014).
In House Advocate/ Children's Rights Officer.	An advocate employed by a local authority.	Children and young people in the care of the specific local authority only. This may include children in need of care and care leavers in that authority area.
Community or Visiting Professional Independent Advocate.	An advocate who is paid or unpaid – working with an independent organisation.	Children, young people and vulnerable adults.
Peer Advocates.	An advocate with similar experiences/personal characteristics to the client.	Young people and vulnerable adults.
Citizen/Informal Advocate.	A befriending advocate who may or may not be linked to an organisation.	Anyone, including children, young people and vulnerable adults.
Independent Domestic Violence Advocate (IDVA).	Specialist advocates who may work across a range of organisations to address the safety of victims and their children.	Vulnerable adults.

Independent Sexual Violence Advocate (ISVA).

Specialist advocates who may work across a range of organisations to address the safety of victims and their children.

Vulnerable adults.

In addition to the statutory IMHA, IMCA and CAA roles, any of the above groups of professional advocates may also be skilled in the non-instructed approach to advocacy.

1.3: Non-instructed advocacy

This is often used with very young children, children or adults with severe learning difficulties, mental health problems or dementia. Non-instructed advocacy requires specific training. This approach should not be employed when working with clients who use alternative communication methods (as explained on the next page). The advocate's role is firstly to check with the client, family and/or professionals to find out how the client would normally communicate.

It is important not to make assumptions that children and adults are always incapable of making decisions and giving instructions. For example, young children and adults with learning difficulties or dementia are often capable of making straightforward decisions but would have difficulty if the issue is complex. In addition some clients may have fluctuating capacity, that is, they may be able to instruct on some occasions but not always due to mental health episodes, medication or illness.

There are several recognised approaches to non-instructed advocacy and it will be useful for all advocates to familiarise themselves with these:

- **Rights-based approach** – the advocate ensures that basic human/legal rights are promoted/upheld.
- **Person-centred approach** – the advocate builds up knowledge of the person, over a period of time and in different environments, so as to put themselves in that person's shoes.
- **Watching brief approach** – the advocate looks at a series of issues and considers how each issue is affected by a key decision.
- **Witness observer approach** – the advocate identifies positive and negative factors, which are then brought to the attention of decision makers.

Although some advocates may choose to use only one of these approaches, other advocates may take a more integrated method. It is always important to be aware of the client's capacity at the point when a decision or instruction is needed. It is then part of the advocate's role to clearly record the method/s used.

1.4: Alternative/augmented communication methods

To be able to express their wishes and feelings it is important that clients are able to use their preferred communication method. For the majority of clients this will be either spoken or written communication in comprehensible English.

When the client has communication impairments or learning disabilities, the advocate needs to be aware of the alternative communication method/s used by the client. Communication methods may include: Makaton, British Sign Language (BSL), Braille, Picture Exchange Communication (PECS), Widgets, plus other specialist computer programs.

For clients who speak very little English, or English as an additional language, an interpreter may be needed. Some statutory and voluntary services employ interpreters to support clients who want to make a complaint or they may agree to pay for an interpreter. There are also specialist language-interpreting phone services where the advocate can speak to the client through an interpreter who is part of the interview.

Advocates may not always have the resources to ensure they meet all their clients' communication needs (e.g. access to an interpreter or PECS) and, in practice, may have to 'make do'. It is important to make every reasonable effort to meet clients' needs and advocates should consider advocating with the service commissioner and their organisation for this, and they should be clear with the client from the outset.

1.5: Advocacy training and qualifications

To achieve best practice, it is important that advocates have up-to-date knowledge and skills. Most advocacy providers require advocates (paid and unpaid) to undertake training and qualifications relevant to their specific role. Some organisations offer their own internal training courses, others have developed training courses accredited by awarding bodies such as Open College Network or Gateway. The national awarding body for advocacy qualifications is City & Guilds.

The City & Guilds IMHA and IMCA qualifications are compulsory for advocates working as statutory Independent Mental Health Advocates and Independent Mental Capacity Advocates.

Advocacy does not have a Level 1 qualification. The Level 2 Award in Independent Advocacy is the introductory level for people who are interested in learning about the independent advocacy role. The Level 3 Certificate in Independent Advocacy and the Level 3 Diploma in Independent Advocacy is for people who are already working as independent advocates either employed or as volunteers. The IMHA and IMCA are specialist units that form part of the certificate and diploma in Independent Advocacy. Also for advocates working in the field of domestic and sexual violence there is an award, certificate and diploma accredited by the Open College Network.

Currently, qualifications are not compulsory for all advocates (except, as noted above, IMHA and IMCA advocates). However, this may change as some commissioners of advocacy services are beginning to take qualifications into account when awarding contracts to advocacy providers.

In relation to independent advocates appointed under the Care Act (2014), the Social Care Institute for Excellence (SCIE) states that they should work towards the Level 3 Certificate in Independent Advocacy within a year of being appointed, and achieve it in a reasonable amount of time thereafter. The qualification is competency-based. For more information see: http://www.scie.org.uk/care-act-2014/advocacy-services/commissioning-independent-advocacy/duties/independent-advocacy-care-act.asp

1.6: Knowledge, skills and attributes needed for the advocacy role

All advocates are different and, in addition to training and qualifications, each advocate is likely to bring unique knowledge, skills and experiences to the role. The advocacy qualifications identify some of the skills and attributes that are considered to be necessary to become a professional advocate. These include (but are not limited to):

- knowledge of relevant legislation and standards
- good communication and interpersonal skills
- good literacy skills

- non-judgmental, person-centred approach
- resilience and persistence
- commitment to promoting equality and diversity
- commitment to empowering individuals.

1.6.1: Knowledge of relevant legislation and standards

Separate chapters in this book will provide advocates and other professionals with the relevant legislation and the statutory basis for making complaints on behalf of clients. Other relevant legislation and guidance will be referenced where necessary.

1.6.2: Good communication and interpersonal skills

Advocacy is a two-way relationship that is built on trust; this is essential and must be at the forefront of the advocate's approach. Advocates must ensure they are listening to and understanding their clients' wishes and feelings. Therefore, active listening skills are needed; these include paraphrasing, asking open and closed questions and accurate summarising. In addition, advocates should also have awareness of their own body language and how this unspoken communication can impact on their clients; there is also the need to be aware of the clients' body language and how this may differ according to age, development, culture, gender or life experiences. Advocates also need good communication skills to successfully liaise and negotiate with complaints' handlers on their client's behalf.

1.6.3: Good literacy skills

Part of the professional advocate's role is to record the client's relevant personal information and thereafter to maintain detailed case records about the work done in relation to the client's complaint. Often advocates (professional or voluntary) will agree to write up the client's formal complaint too. An advocate's tasks may therefore include: completing relevant forms, sending emails, writing formal and informal letters including complaints, writing up case notes and making safeguarding referrals. Furthermore, advocates will need to be able to understand written responses and to quickly digest policies and procedures. Clearly it is essential that advocates have good literacy skills. As nearly all professional advocacy organisations and public institutions routinely use computer systems and databases, it is often expected that advocates will have at least basic information technology skills.

1.6.4: A non-judgmental, person-centred approach

The advocate should maintain a person-centred approach. The client must be the focus at all times. It can sometimes be extremely difficult for the advocate to listen and not disagree with the client, or become overly emotional, especially when the client's wishes do not appear to be in their best interests. For example, children from abusive families often wish to return home and may ask for support from an advocate to submit a complaint that this is not being allowed. Or a vulnerable elderly client might want to continue living independently rather than in a care home. Advocates must be non-judgmental in their approach. Regardless of the advocate's personal view about what is best for the client, it is the client's complaint and this must be submitted and then investigated by the relevant professionals

1.6.5: Resilience and persistence

It follows that advocates won't always agree with their clients' decisions and that the nature of these cases, and sometimes their outcomes, may be deeply distressing for the advocate on a personal and emotional level. Advocates may also sometimes find the decisions of public institutions unfair, unjust or simply upsetting. Although advocates may be well supported by their organisations or by their own family and friends, sometimes advocates will feel overwhelmed and like giving up. Advocates will therefore need a good degree of resilience if they are to maintain their professionalism and to persist in seeking the best outcomes for their clients.

1.6.6: A commitment to promoting equality and diversity

It is part of the advocate's role to use complaints procedures to challenge discrimination, ensuring clients are recognised and respected as individuals. Advocacy organisations must also have policies to promote diversity and equality and should monitor their own services. Advocates should be non-judgmental and respectful of people's needs, wishes, views, culture and experiences.

A client's complaint may be linked to discrimination and therefore advocates should have an awareness of the eight protected characteristics set out in the Equality Act (2010):

- Age.
- Disability.

- Gender reassignment.
- Marriage and civil partnership.
- Pregnancy and maternity.
- Race.
- Religion and belief.
- Sex.
- Sexual orientation.

Further information can be found on the Equality and Human Rights Commission website: www.equalityhumanrights.com/en.

1.6.7: A commitment to empowering individuals

Advocates should always remember that the client has the most knowledge about their own complaints. At the start of the advocacy relationship they are likely to be very reliant on the advocates' skills and knowledge about the complaints process to help them to organise their complaint/s and access the relevant complaints procedure. However, clients should not be viewed as passive individuals who will always need help. As the advocacy relationship continues it is important for the advocate to promote self-empowerment, wherever possible, and to decide with the client if any of the advocacy tasks can be shared.

1.7: Access to advocacy

The majority of advocates are employed by statutory and voluntary organisations. Some agencies offer generic advocacy support and others offer specific advocacy services to groups of clients with particular needs, often related to age and ability. Advocates supporting clients may be paid professionals or unpaid volunteers.

Advocacy services are often commissioned (paid for) by statutory or voluntary organisations to support those in need of advocacy in, for example, their local area, a hospital, a care home or other institution. Professional advocacy support is not available to everyone who wants to make a complaint. Entitlement to advocacy is limited by legislation and funding.

In each chapter of this book, we say whether there is a statutory entitlement to advocacy for different types of complaints. For example, the Children Act 1989 gives 'looked after children', 'children in need' and 'care leavers' the statutory right to advocacy support when making a complaint. This right is not given to all children, only those who are in the categories that are defined in this legislation (see more in Chapter 4).

The Mental Capacity Act (2005) created a scheme to provide an independent mental capacity advocate. The Local Government and Public Involvement in Health Act (2007) states that each local authority must make such arrangements as they consider appropriate for the provision of independent advocacy for complaints about health services (see Chapter 6).

The Care Act (2014) also sets out an entitlement to advocacy for people who meet two specific conditions, or if they are in one of three situations (these are set out in later chapters where they apply). Regardless of entitlement, some local authorities and other institutions will also provide advocacy support even if the complainant does not meet the legal requirements for mandatory professional advocacy support (See Chapter 5).

Advocates should always check if their client is entitled to advocacy. Those often in need of advocacy support and who may be entitled include:

- children and young people wanting support from social care services
- children and young people in the care of a local authority
- children detained in secure accommodation and psychiatric institutions
- children and adults with physical and/or learning disabilities
- children and adults with mental health problems
- vulnerable adults, including the elderly.

1.8: National standards for advocacy organisations

Advocacy organisations and their employees are not subject to formal inspection or formal quality assurance. However, commissioners of advocacy services will often stipulate that advocacy providers must comply with legislation, national standards and guidance. It is therefore important that advocates have a good understanding of the legislation, standards and guidance that relate to their area of advocacy.

As an example, in 2002 the National Standards for the Provision of Children's Advocacy Services was published by the Department of Health. There are ten national standards; each has an explanation of why the standard is important and a list of criteria on how to meet the standard. These standards can be found at: http://webarchive.nationalarchives.gov.uk/20121103024003/http://www.dh.gov.uk/prod_consum_dh/groups/dh_digitalassets/@dh/@en/documents/digitalasset/dh_4018893.pdf

In 2002, Action for Advocacy published the Advocacy Charter. A wide range of advocacy providers working with adults have adopted this charter. The use of the Advocacy Charter resulted in the development of the Quality Standards for Advocacy Scheme in 2006, which contains the principles, quality standards and a code of practice.

'Advocacy is taking action to help people say what they want, secure their rights, represent their interests and obtain services they need. Advocates and advocacy providers work in partnership with the people they support and take their side. Advocacy promotes social inclusion, equality and social justice.' (p.4)

Advocacy QPM is an assessment process that enables some independent advocacy providers to gain a 'quality performance mark' – particularly those who advocate for clients who do not have the perceived mental capacity to make their own decisions.

'Advocates should be clear about the nature and extent of their role. They should understand the boundaries of their own advocacy role and non-advocacy roles such as mediation and advice giving.' (p.7)

The Advocacy Charter, Quality Standards and Code of Practice were revised in 2014 and can be found at: http://www.qualityadvocacy.org.uk/wp-content/uploads/2014/03/Code-of-Practice.pdf

Quality standards continue to be developed for work with specific client groups. The National Institute for Health and Care Excellence (NICE) published quality standards for people supporting adults with dementia in 2013. These include standard 9: *'People with dementia are enabled, with the involvement of their carers, to access independent advocacy services'* (NICE, 2013, p.39). These standards can be found at: https://www.nice.org.uk/guidance/qs30.

1.9: Policies and procedures for advocacy organisations

As well as national standards, it is equally important that advocates have a good understanding of the policies and procedures of the organisation that employs them. It is beyond the scope of this book to list and describe all of those policies or to set out the precise law and guidance that applies in situations such as safeguarding. Good training for advocates is key when it comes to applying these policies and procedures.

Policies and procedures should include (but not be limited to): procedures for complaints from clients, data protection, safeguarding, confidentiality and whistle blowing. If an advocate is working outside of an organisational framework then they will not have these policies but nonetheless should make certain they comply with relevant legislation and familiarise themselves with best practice in the aforementioned areas.

1.9.1: Safeguarding

Safeguarding, in a broad sense, refers to taking steps to protect others from harm or neglect. When an advocate is supporting a child, young person or vulnerable adult it is possible that, in the process of discussing their complaint or reviewing their records, the advocate becomes aware of a safeguarding/protection issue. This means that the advocate may have concerns that their client is at risk of harm due to physical, sexual, emotional or financial abuse or neglect.

Knowledge of the relevant safeguarding legislation, guidance, policies and procedures is paramount. Advocates working with vulnerable clients should ensure they have received adequate safeguarding training to both recognise and handle safeguarding issues. Information may need to be shared with other professionals to ensure the safeguarding of the client and/or other vulnerable children and adults. It is part of the advocate's role to report abuse to the relevant professionals. Depending on the urgency of the issue/s this may be the police or a safeguarding officer at a local authority.

Advocates frequently work with vulnerable clients and so there is a requirement for employed and volunteer advocates to be subjected to the enhanced disclosure and barring police checks.

1.9.2: Confidentiality

Confidentiality refers to what information remains between the client and the advocate or advocacy organisation (and is therefore confidential) and what information may have to be disclosed to other persons or organisations. The advocate and client should set out what information is confidential at the start of the advocacy relationship. It is crucial that the clients understand that an advocate may need to disclose information if there are safeguarding concerns.

As a general principle, it is important that clients trust that the advocate will keep all other information confidential and that they will ask the client for permission when submitting their complaint or before disclosing information to anyone else. It is part of the advocate's role to make sure the information recorded in the complaint is accurate and that the content is exactly what the client wants to disclose within the complaint.

1.9.3: Data protection

When recording and storing clients files, advocates must comply with the eight principles set out in the Data Protection Act (1998):

1. Personal information must be fairly and lawfully processed.
2. Personal information must be processed for limited purposes.
3. Personal information must be adequate, relevant and not excessive.
4. Personal information must be accurate and up-to-date.
5. Personal information must not be kept for longer than is necessary.
6. Personal information must be processed in line with the data subject's rights.
7. Personal information must be secure.
8. Personal information must not be transferred abroad without protection.

Advocates must be familiar with data protection legislation and the policy and procedures of their own organisation for data use and storage. When creating client records always check the spelling of the client's name, the correct order of names (first, middle, last etc.) and if the client uses, or has used, a different name. Accurate and up-to-date recording of the client's date of birth and address is necessary to ensure records do not get mixed up.

1.9.4: Lone working, risk assessments and personal boundaries

Advocates often work on their own when speaking with or visiting clients. Whether meeting face-to-face or by phone it is important that advocates consider any risks that may exist to themselves and to the client. The advocate and client may be at risk should they meet in certain locations because of the client's (previous or current) involvement in gangs or relationship with an abusive partner, for example. The advocate should also consider risk if the client has a known history of violence against others or themselves or if the client has made previous adverse allegations against professionals or volunteers (note that this latter example can occur through a phone contact). Often no such risk exists but advocates should make all reasonable efforts to be sure. Sometimes this may involve seeking the client's consent to discuss any risks with other professionals or volunteers, with whom the client has already worked. Advocates should then take practicable steps to manage any identified risks. This may mean agreeing to meet the client in a certain safe place or agreeing to meet the client in pairs (i.e. with another advocate).

Sometimes it will not be possible to speak to anyone with whom the client has previously worked, and in any case, there is no guaranteed method of identifying all risks. Advocates should therefore be aware of general precautions they can always take. When visiting any client outside of their own offices, advocates should make sure that either their organisation or a colleague/friend/family member is aware of the exact time and place of the visit. They should report back to someone after the visit. Advocates should be mindful of verbal and non-verbal cues of their client and seek to end meetings where clients become abusive or seem intoxicated. In face-to-face meetings, advocates should seat themselves near an exit, so that they can easily leave if they feel threatened, but should be careful never to block the exit from the client (as feeling 'trapped' can exacerbate the client's temper should the client wish to leave).

It is important to note that risk assessment is an on-going process and not something that only happens at the beginning of the advocacy relationship.

Finally, advocates must ensure that they do not cross personal boundaries with clients. This is a particularly difficult issue and there are no set rules, although some organisations will have particular policies. All advocates should be aware of the client's vulnerability. For instance an advocate should think in advance about their boundaries in relation to physical contact, the giving and receiving of gifts, the use of social media/personal mobile phones to make contact, out of hours contact and the frequency of contact.

1.9.5: Supervision

Supervision/line management provides a measure of quality assurance for the client, the organisation and the advocate. Skilled supervision is a necessary support for professional and voluntary advocates. Supervision helps to ensure that individual advocates maintain their role and the boundaries of their involvement with the client and other professionals. Sometimes it is possible for boundaries to become blurred. This can occur if the advocate becomes too emotionally involved with the client, or over-empathises with the professionals when the client has challenging behaviour and is difficult to work with.

Supervision should focus on casework and also provide space to address the advocate's well-being and continuing professional development. If a client makes a complaint about the advocate, the supervisor's records can be useful for any investigation process.

Depending on the organisation, the supervision may be individual or in a group. Sometimes supervision is done by telephone contact. The level of supervision will often depend on the size of the advocate's caseload and the organisation's funding. Supervisors should have a good understanding of the advocate's skills, abilities and workload in order to be able to offer challenges and support. In addition to formal supervision, advocates often set up peer support groups; these can provide ongoing advice and support between supervision sessions or when supervision isn't provided.

It is part of the advocate's role to contact the supervisor/line manager if they need advice and guidance in between regular supervision sessions.

1.10: The limits of the advocacy role

Many children, young people and vulnerable adults will have experienced trauma and abuse in their lives. It can be very difficult for advocates to listen to graphic accounts of cruelty, abandonment, abuse and neglect, especially when these problems appear to have been compounded by a lack of services and support from institutions and key professionals. It can also be tough when advocates see their clients striving to carry out simple daily tasks and their general struggle to cope with life. To support the client the advocate must maintain a professional empathetic approach.

It is not the advocate's role to become the client's counsellor, keyworker or therapist. Parts of a client's complaint may relate to what the client has, or is still suffering, but the advocate's focus must be to ensure the substantive issues in client's grievances are being duly investigated and resolved. Advocates may also signpost clients to alternative, more appropriate services. Sometimes the advocate may even be able to assist the client in requesting service provision, such as therapeutic support, as an outcome of a complaint.

The limits of the advocacy role can be extremely frustrating for advocates but it is important to consider that advocacy and advocates play a vital part in helping their clients, and advocates cannot do this well if they are too busy taking on the roles of other professionals.

1.11: Obtaining legal advice

Advocates are not normally qualified lawyers but they are offering guidance in relation to complaint systems, which have the full force of the law, and in these circumstances, they are advising in relation to legal matters. This may come as a surprise to some advocates and advocacy organisations, but it must be the case, given that so often complaints are about the denial of a legal right.

All advocates should maintain an awareness of the potential need to refer a client to expert legal advice at any point in the case. It may be very difficult for advocates to recognise this kind of situation but at the same time it is important to realise the limits of one's capability. One example might be a situation where emergency action is required, such as a local authority decision to remove children from a placement against their wishes. Another example might be a child or an adult who is homeless. It may be any situation where there is an extremely short time frame or where the significance of what is happening is particularly serious, or where the matter is very complex. There are no hard and fast rules about when to seek legal advice but experience is very helpful. Very often the advocate may simply find that they are 'stuck'.

In the writers' experience, it can be very helpful for an advocate to have knowledge of, or maintain a relationship with, lawyers' firms that specialise in various areas. It is vital to obtain the client's consent before approaching an outside party and to record that consent.

Many law firms will provide free advice if asked. That process can add enormously to an advocate's experience, knowledge and confidence. Many firms are happy to spend a little time with advocates on the telephone and actively maintain links with advocacy organisations as well as supporting them. At the same time, the presentation of the case by the advocate to the lawyer is something that the client (particularly if they are a child) simply may not be able to do. Consequently the advocate may be the only means by which a client obtains access to justice.

1.12: Key points

- There are many different types of advocate and roles may differ according to specialism.
- Clients are likely to be vulnerable and therefore appropriate communication is essential.
- Advocates must comply with all relevant legislation, guidance and national and organisational standards.
- Specialised qualifications are compulsory for Independent Mental Health Advocates, Independent Mental Capacity Advocates and Care Act Advocates.
- A fundamental part of advocacy is to listen, to understand the reasons for the complaint and to know what outcomes the client wants.

NEGLIGENCE
FAILURE
ABUSE
INJUSTICE
NEGLECT
DISCRIMINATION
EDUCATION
EQUALITY
SOCIAL CARE
PROTECTION
COMPENSATION
PALS
CHILD SAFET
HUMAN RIGHTS
WHEN TO INSTRUCT A LAWYER
JUSTICE
DUTY OF CARE
THE TASK OF THE ADVOCATE
THE LAWS OF ENGLAND
A. HOPE

Chapter 2: The tasks of the advocate

2.1: Overview

Now that the advocacy role has been explained we turn to the tasks of the advocate. Advocates may have many different personal motivations and aims. They may be driven by a desire to seek justice, to empower their clients, to address systemic failures, and to feel that they have made a difference. A professional advocate may also need to consider an on-going organisational relationship with a specific institution. An informal advocate may be driven by their wish to see a loved one or friend's situation improved. However the ultimate and prevailing task of the advocate when making a complaint is to achieve the best outcome for their client, in other words, the outcome that the client wants. The tasks of the advocate are often dictated by the type of complaint. This chapter will examine the advocacy process and the tasks an advocate should undertake in order to successfully navigate the different complaints procedures and achieve their client's desired outcomes.

2.2: The referral

Advocacy referrals come in many shapes and forms. Advocacy referrals may be accepted in writing or verbally or by a prescribed form. Referrals will usually include basic information such as: name, gender, date of birth, address, contact details, legal status, any communication or access needs, any information pertaining to risk (of working with that client), and a basic outline of their grievance. As soon as possible it is important to check the accuracy of the client's name/s, what they prefer to be called, their date of birth and address.

Depending on age and ability, a client may self-refer or be referred by a friend or family member or by a professional who has recognised the need for the person to have the support of an independent advocate. Some institutions have contracts with independent advocacy services to provide advocacy for their clients. Advocacy organisations will nearly always have eligibility rules covering a range of criteria such as age, location, and legal status. In some institutions, clients may automatically have access to a resident or visiting advocate. When a referral is made organisations will usually do their best to match the advocate to any preferences the client has, such as gender, but this is not always possible. As explained in Chapter 1, access to professional advocacy varies widely; there are certain groups of people who have a legal right to advocacy when making a complaint against specific institutions. However sometimes advocacy provision may depend entirely on the availability of charities or community organisations.

The more detailed the referral, the better equipped the advocate will be when meeting or speaking with the client for the first time. However, it is also important to ensure that advocacy is widely available and sometimes this will mean organisations must accept that referrers may not have the skills or time to provide a detailed referral. Accordingly it is important to treat referrals as guides to the client's wishes and situation, upon which the advocate needs to build.

Not all advocacy referrals will be about complaints and sometimes a formal complaint may not be the best way of reaching the client's desired outcome. Advocates should avoid making assumptions about what the client wants until they have had the opportunity to speak to the client and learn more. It is important for advocates to be able to recognise when a client may be in an urgent situation for which the complaints process is not the most appropriate route. In these circumstances the client might need to be supported or signposted to access a lawyer and legal support.

Every client is different. Some clients are very clear about what they want to complain about. There are clients who do not know about their right to complain. Occasionally, clients have inadvertently started the complaints process; for example, the client might not be aware that a verbal complaint they have made has been accepted as a formal complaint. Clients can often have unrealistic expectations about what the complaints process can achieve. When they are better informed some do not wish to continue and others may decide to pursue alternative routes to resolution. Regardless of the advocate's view it is the client's decision about when and how to proceed with their complaint. However, it is also important that the advocate makes the client aware if there is a timescale attached to the given complaints process.

2.3: Planning the initial meeting

It is usually best practice to hold the initial meeting with the client in person. However, this may not always be possible and sometimes the initial meeting may be by telephone. The importance of this meeting cannot be underestimated and it is vital to plan it well. Advocates should make sure they are aware of the client's communication needs. If an interpreter is used the advocate should check not only that the client understands the interpreter, but also that they are satisfied the interpreter is directly translating their client's words. The referral may indicate that the client uses alternative or augmented forms of communication; all practicable and reasonable efforts should be made to accommodate these. The advocate should also consider if there is likely to be any expected communication obstructions – for example, if the client is a young child the advocate would need to adjust the level of language appropriately and/or consider breaking the meeting into two parts.

If the initial meeting is by phone, advocates should aim to ensure they consider in advance that their client will be somewhere quiet for the duration of the phone call, will be alert (for example, do they take medication at a certain time of day), will be able to talk freely (away from other people); will have a full battery and good reception.

If the initial meeting is to be in person the advocate should check, in advance, to see if there are any risks for the advocate and/or client if they meet alone. If there are identified risks it may be necessary to hold the first meeting in a private but safe space such as a room in the advocacy organisation's office or another institution where security is available. Sometimes the client may ask the advocate to visit them in their own home, or in a community venue, for example a library or cafe. There are clients who have to be visited in formal settings such as care homes, mental health units, schools or prisons. Visiting times may be limited. Therefore, advocates should prepare for such visits in advance and check the organisations visiting procedures and what documentation they require from the advocate. They may need to provide the organisation with evidence of an up-to-date disclosure and barring (DBS) check, or have other security checks carried out. Regardless of the meeting setting, advocates should always carry their professional ID or, if this is not possible, another form of identification to show to the client. It can be useful to ask the client to bring their ID and if it is feasible, to take photocopies. It can also be useful for advocates to bring a consent form for the client to sign. Proof of consent and identity is sometimes required by institutions before they will give the advocate access to information it holds on the client.

When the initial meeting date, time and venue have been agreed it is helpful to confirm this using the client's confirmed communication method. For some this may be email, letter, text or a specialist method.

Many advocacy organisations have some type of initial agreement form. These forms will often include:

- the client's personal details
- the client's preferred method/s of communication
- the advocate's name and contact details
- a summary of the advocacy role
- availability of client and advocate
- expectations of both advocate and client
- outline of the client's issues
- outline of the client's desired outcomes
- confidentiality and safeguarding
- data protection
- the advocacy organisation's own complaint process.

The initial meeting can often be overwhelming for the client, either emotionally or because of the sheer amount of information shared. Advocates need to use their professional judgment on a case-by-case basis about the most appropriate way to organise the initial meeting. Some clients prefer to start the meeting factually by getting the form-filling 'out of the way' others want to concentrate on their complaint issues and leave forms until the end of the meeting. It can be useful for the advocate to have a prompt sheet to ensure that all the relevant points and procedures are covered in the meeting.

Advocates should consider how they will introduce or start the meeting. With experience, most advocates will develop a basic text in their head that can be adapted to the individual client.

For example:

'Hello … it's nice to see you today and thank you for meeting with me. Before we start talking about your issues I'm going to explain a little bit about what my role is and everything we need to do in the meeting today. We have already agreed on … hours for this meeting and hopefully this will give us enough time to talk about your complaints and complete all of the forms to make sure I have the information I need to help you. If you don't understand anything or want to ask questions please ask as we go along. At times I might have to interrupt you as

well. I might need to clarify certain bits of information or to make sure I have got dates or names right. When you have explained everything we can then talk about your options and what the next steps are for both of us. If you would like a break at any time just let me know. I will also give you some information on your rights and explain how they apply to what you have told me. I will also explain/give you information about confidentiality, safeguarding, data protection and how you can complain to my organisation if you are not satisfied with my work. After the meeting I will make sure you have copies of any information you need.'

2.4: The advocacy process

Although there are various types of advocate and advocacy, the advocacy process can be stripped down to an essential cycle. Once understood, the advocate will be able to transfer this process to the specific client's complaint/s. The following sections refer to instructed advocacy (that is where the client is able to instruct their client although they may need assistance by way of an interpreter or they have may have alternative or augmented communication needs). We have discussed non-instructed advocacy in the previous chapter and reiterate that it is important for advocates to seek specialist training if providing non-instructed advocacy.

2.4.1: Build trust

The advocacy relationship is based on trust. All clients who want the support of an advocate will be hindered in advocating for themselves in some way. It may be, for example, that they have a disability that prevents them from expressing their views directly, or a mental health condition that prevents them from understanding or processing information, or if they are very young or old with memory difficulties it may mean that they do not have the capacity to weigh up complex arguments. Some clients will be unable to advocate for themselves because they lack confidence to complain against an institution on their own. Others may have complained previously but have not felt their complaint has been heard. Clients need to trust their advocates to take on their complaint as this often means sharing very personal information.

In every meeting and interaction with the client there may be numerous issues to work through: explaining the advocacy role, confidentiality, safeguarding, boundaries, providing an update, gathering information. Professional advocates may have time restraints or forms that need to be filled in. It is important to always remember that the client is an individual person and not just a case; it is vital that advocates expend just as much effort on their 'soft' skills as they do learning about the various relevant laws, procedures, guidelines and other policies.

Many books have been written on how to build rapport and trust. However there is really no substitute for experience and self-critical reflection. Clients will start testing how trustworthy the advocate is from the very first interaction. The importance of active listening cannot be overstated. Advocates should not be afraid to interrupt clients if they haven't understood something, so long as they explain the interruption. Advocates should also encourage clients to interrupt if they don't understand something; they should give clients time to think and not feel a need to fill silences. Advocates should be alert to clients' emotional and physical well-being – offering breaks when appropriate or even suggesting a meeting be continued on another day.

The advocacy relationship should be transparent – advocates should make clear that they will not keep information from their clients (this should also be made clear to professionals who want to share information without the client's knowledge). Many clients feel they have been let down by other professionals and therefore reliability is essential. Advocates should try to be on time for appointments and keep to schedule. However, if things don't go to plan, advocates should be honest with clients and update them as soon as possible. Advocates should never make promises about anything, ever, other than that they will do their best.

Trust goes both ways. It is helpful if clients are also clear about the expectations advocates have of them. For clients who are especially vulnerable there may be minimal expectations or, for example in the case of non-instructed advocacy, no obligations at all. However, for the majority of cases, advocates should make it clear that they expect their clients to be honest, contactable, non-abusive, and that they will provide their advocate with any important information about their case as it progresses.

2.4.2: Gather information

Gathering information from the client is often the hardest task the advocate faces. Advocates will often have a limited time to commit to a meeting with their client and may also be restricted in the number/frequency of meetings they can arrange. There may be any number of communication obstacles. Clients may struggle to clearly and concisely explain their grievance for any number of reasons, including but not limited to: their distress, their vulnerability, their age, their language ability, their special educational needs, their disability, and their confidence. The advocate will have to reach a delicate balance of listening empathetically and directing the meeting so that all necessary information pertinent to the potential complaint is obtained. This will often mean sensitively interrupting the client to cut short repeated information or to ask further questions for clarification. Sometimes it may mean having to think creatively about how to elicit more substantial responses. It is useful to advise the client about how the meeting will be recorded; whether notes will be typed or handwritten and how the client can contribute to their accuracy. Being clear about the advocacy approach from the start of the meeting will also help to foster trust.

Of course, much of the information the advocate needs will depend on the content of the grievance and the institution complained about. Clients rightfully expect professional advocates to be up-to-date with any relevant legislation or guidance. However there is some information that may be considered generally useful to making complaints.

Creating a precise chronology of events can be vital for some complaints, especially if the grievance relates to a number of minor decisions/actions/ omissions over a period of time. This can assist the client and advocate in getting a sense of the potential complaint as a whole and helps the advocate to identify relevant documents and the professionals involved. It will also assist the complaint handler when the complaint has been submitted. If the complaint concerns an omission by an institution to act within the appropriate timeframe, then the chronology will evidence this. A good chronology should also evidence any attempts the client has made to resolve the issue before bringing a formal complaint. It is essential, in particular, to know the date of the incident or decision complained of because most complaints procedures stipulate specific time-frames within which complaints need to be submitted. If a complaint is submitted outside of this time frame, then a chronology can help to argue any compelling reasons for a delay.

Gathering information about what evidence there may be to substantiate their client's grievance is a necessary task. Questioning should be done sensitively and clients may need reassurance that advocates are asking questions because they want to help and not because they do not believe their client. It is good practice to develop the habit of asking a client how they know something happened and if they know the date. Were they there and if so who else was there? Did they receive an email/letter/phone call and if so from whom?

As previously stated, advocates should always ask the client to provide them with all documents which are relevant to their complaint. However, clients may not always be aware of precisely which documents are relevant and the advocate should always seek to clarify if there are any more potentially useful documents. They may mention electronic communications such as emails or texts, which they still hold. The client may not have considered receipts or bank statements as potential sources of evidence. The client may or may not be aware that the institution holds certain documents or records relevant to the complaint. If the complaint relates to discussions or meetings held with professionals then it is possible that written records can be requested. If the client has been known to the advocacy organisation before then these records may be a useful source of evidence.

It is also important to keep a record of the names and contact details of any of the institution's officers or other professionals who are mentioned by the client and are relevant to the complaint. The advocate may prefer to do this as each officer is mentioned one-by-one by the client or to seek contact information at the end of the meeting. In some cases clients are not aware of the overarching institution they are complaining about. For example, children often know they are in care, but not the name of the local authority that is responsible for their care. Some clients know they want to complain about a hospital but will not know which trust the hospital is in. Even when clients know the name of the institution they may not always have full names or contact details of officers but the more information they can provide the better; this is because the client and advocate may agree to seek further clarifying information from some or all of these officers before submitting a complaint.

All clients are individuals and some may be very willing and able to reflect on how the institutions' decisions, actions or omissions have affected them whereas other clients may need prompting to articulate this. Advocates should certainly seek to clarify their clients' feelings. This will help them to understand which aspects of the complaint are most important to the client and should be prioritised. It will also help to breathe life into the complaint, assisting the complaint handler in building a full picture of the complaint and complainant. Moreover, it is important to clearly present, in the complaint, the impact of the institution's decisions, actions or omissions on the client because this will indicate the seriousness of the institution's failure and consequently will feed into the remedy. Advocates should constantly be alert to:

- Any emotional or psychological distress suffered – particularly if it has led to a medical diagnosis of ill health and this link can be evidenced.

- Monetary loss – has the client had to take time off work to deal with the issue? Have they had to spend money for provision of a service, which they feel should have been provided by the institution? Again, clarify what evidence the client has for any monetary loss.

- Any loss of liberty, shelter, livelihood – or other such serious life-changing losses. If the client feels that the institution's failures have led to any of these then this should be explicitly stated to reflect the gravity of the complaint.
- Any breach of human rights. The European Convention on Human Rights has been reproduced in English law by the Human Rights Act (1998) and advocates should make themselves aware of its provisions if supporting clients to complain against public bodies.

Human Rights Act (1998) – the main articles

- The right to life (Article 2).
- Freedom from torture (Article 3).
- Freedom from slavery (Article 4).
- The right to liberty (Article 5).
- The right to a fair trial (Article 6).
- The right to respect for family and private life (Article 8).
- The right not to be discriminated against (Article 14).
- The right to education (Protocol 1, Article 2).

Advocates are often asked – 'how much can I claim?' It is important to explain to a client that the advocate cannot force the institution to make a particular award or take particular action and that, just because a case appears similar to another case, it does not mean that the award or action taken in that case will be taken in the client's case. There are always a whole host of variables. The advocate needs to bear in mind that compensation and other remedies are assessed on a case-by-case basis and it may be impossible to fit the client's circumstances to any one case. However, the writers would encourage advocates to do their research and see if there are any cases (from examples on the Ombudsman's websites) which can guide them. In later chapters, we provide brief summaries of such cases.

It is important to try and pin down the specific decisions, acts or omissions, about which the client is complaining. Try to break each complaint down into its simplest form such as: decision to do X on X date, X action on X date, failure to do X on X date. Then, as the advocate is coming to the end of gathering information, list all the complaints and repeat them back to the client to check they fairly reflect the client's views. Once both client and advocate are happy with the list of complaints then the advocate should make sure they have accurately reflected the impact each specific decision, action or omission has had on the client and opportunity to talk with their family and/or friends. Sometimes clients may want help to understand the pros and cons of each option – this is fine but advocates must take care not to cross the fine line into advice/telling them what to do. Sometimes the client may have competing priorities or problems in their life – following a formal complaint process can be emotionally draining and advocates should make sure the client feels comfortable to walk away from the complaints process if they are not ready for it, for whatever reason.

Clients can also worry that submitting a complaint will make matters worse for them; their concern is that professionals will be angry about being questioned or criticised. Advocates cannot promise this won't be the case, though in the authors' experience this is unusual. Ultimately, the client must make the choice that is right for them at that point in their life but advocates can offer the reassurance that the client will have the support of an advocate if they do decide to make a complaint.

2.4.4: Agree the next steps

Once the client has made their decision, the advocate can discuss the next steps. These should be clear and time specific as a general rule. If it is agreed that more information is required before the complaint will be submitted then it should be agreed who is responsible for gathering which information and by when. The advocate and client should agree to whom the complaint will be submitted; the client may wish the complaint to go directly and solely to the relevant complaints manager or may wish other officers in the institution to be advised ahead or following the complaint's submission. If the complaint concerns a decision/action/omission that is likely to take place in the near future, it may be worth discussing with the client whether to submit an initial verbal complaint with a written complaint to follow.

With regards to writing the complaint, if the complaint does not require an urgent response, advocates should aim to set generous but reasonable timescales. It is better to exceed a generous timescale then to be late for an optimistic one. It is good practice for the client to be able to review the complaint before it is submitted. Client and advocate should discuss how this will be done; it could be by email, could be read over the phone or could be posted. If the advocate does not intend to submit the complaint until receiving positive confirmation from the client then this should be made clear to the client. Alternatively, if the client is sure that they do not want to review the written complaint, then advocates should be doubly certain that they have understood their client's situation, wishes and feelings. Some institutions will not accept complaints unless they have been counter-signed by the client.

By the end of every meeting with the advocate the client should know approximately when they will hear from the advocate next. They should also know how to contact the advocate if they have any news to share relating to the complaint and they should know who they can contact should they be unable to contact their own allocated advocate. Regular feedback to the client fosters trust but advocates must also respect that clients may have other commitments and likewise, should ensure their clients are aware of their own availability. Advocates may wish to consider writing a brief letter or email to the client, outlining the content of their meeting and outlining the next steps.

2.5: Presenting a complaint

Advocates will develop their own unique style and method of presenting a complaint, as each hones their own skills and uses their individual experiences and knowledge. Some advocacy organisations also have preferred formats for presenting complaints. Nonetheless, advocates would do well to consider the following guidance.

2.5.1: Keep it formal

As a rule of thumb, complaints should always be presented in writing as a letter and not set out in an email. Although some straightforward and simple grievances may be able to be resolved verbally, it is good to have a written record of both the complaint and of any written response. This can be useful if an issue repeats itself in the future or if an agreed resolution is not actioned within a given or reasonable time frame. Advocates will then have written evidence to hold the institution to account. Some institutions will have their own complaints forms, which they may encourage advocates and clients to use when submitting complaints. The potential harm in using a complaints form is that, as many of these are online, it is not always clear from the start how and where the record of the complaint will be kept. If in any doubt, it is prudent to submit a complaint letter in addition to any form.

The written complaint should be presented as a formal document. It should follow a formal letter template and be signed and dated. If the letter is being sent from a professional advocacy organisation, it should ideally be presented on headed paper. Although a hard copy should be sent in the post, it is often a good idea to send a copy by fax or email (using a secure system) for speed. Advocates should take care that they have the correct contact details. If sending a document by email, advocates should, whenever possible, send it as a pdf file or some other format that cannot be edited by the recipient. Be alive to issues raised in the previous chapter around data protection.

The tone throughout the letter should be professional. Being professional does not mean trying to use long and technical words. Indeed it is better to avoid acronyms and industry jargon. Bear in mind that, for the most part, clients will want to review the letter before it is submitted so letters should be written in such a way that the client will also understand. Advocates should use clear, straightforward English – no slang words, text abbreviations or emojis (unless clearly quoting). Be sure to proof read the complaint at least once for readability, spelling and grammar. Some advocacy organisations/managers want to read all complaints before they are submitted.

The most important aspect of striking a professional tone is to remain fair-minded, reasonable and objective. If the client is grateful for the help or efforts made by any part of the institution, either currently or historically, then it's worth including this. Steer clear of over-emotive language, personal attacks and unsubstantiated accusations. When advocates start to get angry or upset, it can come through in the complaint letter – in these circumstances advocates would be wise to take a break and come back to writing once calmed down. Even very experienced advocates can become over-involved and emotional when there appears to be ample evidence of injustice to the client. Remember that, ultimately, the person who will be reading and handling the complaint has to be presented with a clear summary of the client's complaint/s. Advocates need that person to consider the complaint sympathetically if they are to achieve their client's desired outcomes. An overly emotional complaint tends to elicit overly defensive responses.

2.5.2: Remember the complainant

It should always be clear that the advocate is presenting a complaint on behalf of the client; this should be stated clearly in the opening of any complaint letter and at the beginning of any correspondence or communication with professionals involved in the complaint. Formal advocates should state which organisation they are from and, if applicable, a very brief summary of the legal basis for their advocacy work. Informal advocates (friends and family) should state their relationship to the client and also, briefly, the reason why they are advocating for them. Advocates should also provide a form of authority or consent form, signed and dated by the client, which allows the institution to share information about the client with the advocate or advocacy organisation. Taking these simple initial steps will help prevent any disputes about the advocate's right to act on behalf of their client.

Public bodies and private companies tend to have complex systems in place to record their interactions with individual members of the public, understandably most ordinary people do not keep any such records. Complaint handlers will be aware of this when looking into the complaint and make allowances for it. However it is important that advocates, in the body of the complaint, avoid assertions they cannot prove. In other words, if the only evidence that something happened/didn't happen is that the client says so, then make sure the complaint reflects this. Use phrases such as 'X said, X states, X reports, X recalls, X thinks'. This is a very important habit to develop as it is useful in preventing an unnecessary back-and-forth about providing evidence where evidence is limited. Of course, if the client does have evidence about any of their assertions, then refer to this in the complaint and provide this evidence or copies of it alongside the complaint.

Consider using the client's own words about their wishes and feelings wherever appropriate and suitable, being sure to make it clear where doing so. Using the client's voice will help both the advocate and the complaint handler to keep the client in mind. Furthermore it helps the complaint handlers to better relate to and understand the client, which can be vital if the client will have an ongoing relationship with that institution after the complaint has been resolved. On a human level, it is more compelling and interesting for the complaint handler to read a complaint with a bit of a personality – they are likely to prioritise resolving a complaint where there is a real person at the bottom of it.

2.5.3: The layout of the complaint

Think carefully about the layout of the complaint letter and try to consider it from the point of view of the complaint handler. Think about what would make the complaint easy for the complaint handler to understand. Consider dividing the complaint into clear headings, thinking about what information the complaint handler will need to have to resolve the grievance. At the very least a well laid-out complaint should include:

- introduction
- background to the complaints
- rights/law relevant to the complaints
- specific complaints
- desired outcomes – what the client wants to happen as a result of the complaint.

Keep the complaint as concise as possible. Some complaints will be long, spanning several pages – make sure the pages are numbered and consider whether the paragraphs need to be numbered too.

Introduction: sets out the advocate's relationship to the client and introduces the client. Provides a summary of the complaint, this need not be more than a sentence or two. Highlights any urgent information such as decisions that require immediate freezing or any request for an accelerated response.

Background: provides a chronological background of the client (as far as is relevant to their complaint) and of their interactions with the organisation/ professionals they are complaining about up to the date of the complaint. It may also be useful to set out how the client has been affected by any of the institutions decisions, actions or omissions.

Rights/law: sets out the relevant rights of the client. This may include any relevant laws, guidance or policies relating to the complaints. It should try to show how these have not been followed.

Specific complaints: clearly sets out the actual specific complaints. Where there are several complaints these should be numbered to avoid a partial or incomplete response.

Desired outcomes: clearly sets out the client's desired outcomes. Where there are several desired outcomes these should be numbered to avoid a partial or incomplete response.

At the end of the letter make sure that the deadline for a response is clear. If requesting an accelerated response make sure that the reasons for this are also clear.

2.6: Progressing the complaint

In ideal circumstances, once a complaint is submitted, the institution will respond within the prescribed time frame with a letter that addresses all of the points raised in the client's complaint and which accepts the client's desired outcomes. If this is done then the client is likely to be satisfied; there will be little else for the advocate to do other than to keep in mind the advocacy process when feeding back to the client. However such an ideal scenario is unusual and in the majority of cases the advocacy tasks do not end after the initial complaint is submitted. In the first instance, timescales are frequently missed. If the client is not satisfied with the institution's response to the complaint then the advocate should provide the client with further options in getting their complaints resolved. What happens next will be dependent on the institution's complaints procedure. If the client wants to escalate their complaint through the formal stages the advocate should keep in mind the advocacy process – building trust, gathering information, providing information and agreeing the next steps. The advocate should also be aware of how to manage and explain aspects of the complaint process, which the client is likely to encounter. Some complaints procedures involve a formal panel hearing which clients may find daunting.

2.6.1: Keeping records

We have touched upon the importance of keeping records already. Records may be useful to the client's current complaint or any future complaints, as they act as evidence of decisions, actions or omissions of the institution, by which the institution may be held to account. Furthermore, as the information advocates hold on clients is frequently of a sensitive and confidential nature, the advocate has a duty as a data processor to keep accurate, reliable records for the benefit of the client, who has the right to request access to this information at any time. Those working in professional advocacy organisations may be required to keep accurate records for the purpose of supervision, complaints about the organisation, monitoring, commissioning and service quality assurance. Records to be kept should usually include: any documents (or copies) provided by the client, the complaint and any responses, e-mails and other written correspondence with the client or institution, notes from any meetings or phone calls with the client or institution. Organisations should have data protection policies clearly setting out which information is stored, how long for, and how the client may have access to it.

2.6.2: Chasing responses

Complaint handlers do their best to respond to complaints or other correspondences within reasonable or prescribed time frames but they do not always achieve this. Often, particularly at the first stage of the complaint, it will be a front-line worker putting most of the effort into answering the complaint, and this worker is likely to be already managing a heavy case load of other tasks. This, of course, does not mean that the client should expect anything less than a prompt and timely response. However advocates who manage to get a balance between persistence and understanding of limited resources will achieve the best outcomes for their clients.

Advocates should clearly state where they are expecting a response by a certain deadline and, if there is one, should outline the statutory basis for this prescribed deadline. They should seek agreement at the outset that the complaint handler will respond by this deadline. In situations where the complaint needs a swifter resolution because of some crisis (for example, if a client is facing homelessness or is to be moved from a placement), this should be clearly explained and the advocate should attempt to seek a reasonable resolution with the complaint handler about timescales. Advocates should be open to compromise (of course with the caveat that all decisions will need to be made with their client); sometimes a complaint handler might agree certain concessions or requests at the outset if the complainant agrees a longer period for a full response.

Advocates should have agreed with their clients about the level of contact to be made once the complaint is submitted and whether the client wants to receive every update or just significant updates; advocates should not make unilateral decisions when chasing responses unless given this permission by the client.

Advocates should give complaint handlers reasonable time to respond to correspondence. At the same time, advocates should recognise when their attempts to get a response are not working and should have the confidence and competence to successfully escalate the matter. It is good practice to ask at the beginning of the complaint if there are any days of the week on which the complaints' handler doesn't work, there are any planned annual leave days in the time frame or just after the time frame for a response, and who to contact if the advocate cannot get hold of the complaint handler for whatever reason (for example, if the complaint handler takes unexpected sick leave). If possible, it is also good to set up expectations for correspondence – for example, can the complaint handler agree to respond to voicemails within one working day, simple emails within two, and complex emails within one week? In return, advocates should be clear if they only work part-time and also try to be consistent and prompt in their own responses. Even when overworked, which will inevitably happen at points, it is good practice to respond promptly if only to acknowledge correspondence and to be upfront if you will be delayed in providing a meaningful response.

All of the above, of course, requires that the advocate develops a good system of checking their correspondence regularly and highlighting important deadlines. For some complaints systems, there are prescribed deadlines for the client to escalate the complaint to the next stage of the procedure, so it is doubly important in these instances for the advocate to be 'on top of' their calendar and record the date when the complaint was received and the date when a response to the complaint can be expected.

2.6.3: Attending meetings

Institutions may sometimes attempt to investigate or resolve complaints by offering the client a meeting with the complaint handler and/or any persons relevant to the complaint. If the advocate has made the complaint on behalf of the client, it is usual for the advocate to be invited however this does not always happen. This is one of the reasons why it is so important that the advocate and client set out at the beginning to keep each other informed of important developments. If a meeting is offered as part of the complaints process, the client has the right to ask for their advocate to attend. Clients are not obliged to go to meetings but it is a usually a good idea to try to cooperate as fully as possible. Advocates are not obliged to attend these meetings too but this is usually the part of the complaints process that is most intimidating to clients. It is good practice for advocates to make themselves available, or if they can't attend, and it is feasible, to ask the client if they would like a substitute advocate to go in their place.

Institutions should make reasonable efforts to hold any meetings at a time and place that is convenient for the client (and advocate, should the client wish the advocate to attend); they should also make sure that all practicable steps are made with regards to access requirements and any communication needs. It should be clear, in advance of the meeting, what the agenda and intended outcome of the meeting is. Where possible, any documents that will be considered in the meeting should be made available to the client and advocate in advance.

The advocate should make sure they set sufficient time aside to prepare for the meeting with their client. They should agree the extent of support in the meeting, for example; does the client want the advocate to do all the talking; does the client want to try to talk but to have a cue for help if they falter, does the client only want the advocate to interrupt entirely at the advocate's discretion? The client and advocate should be clear about any points they definitely want to raise (and if there is a long list consider writing these down). They should also have a good idea of what the client hopes to achieve from the meeting.

It is always a good idea for the advocate to take notes during the meeting, even where there is a minute-taker, although the focus on the meeting should clearly be the client and not detailed minute-taking. It can also be useful to send a copy or a typed-up version of the advocate's notes to other participants so that the accuracy can be verified as soon as possible (particularly important where there are any points of contention).

A meeting that is well-run will ensure that the client understands what is happening, that they are given due opportunity to speak, and that everyone is professional and courteous throughout. When this isn't happening, the advocate should not be afraid of interrupting to ask for clarification of specialist terminology, to ask for opportunity for the client to speak (or to speak on behalf of the client), or to challenge misinformation, discourteous comments or otherwise unacceptable behaviour. The advocate will need to be assertive but polite to intervene effectively in this way. The advocate should also maintain an awareness of their client's level of distress/tiredness/anger and be prepared to ask for a break. Advocates should remember that they act as role models to their clients in these meetings (as well as representatives of their respective advocacy organisations) and should act in a way that fosters respect, cooperation and confidence. They should also, where appropriate, try to use this opportunity to help empower their client.

After the meeting, wherever possible and if the client wishes it, the advocate should aim to spend time with the client to talk over what went well and what didn't go so well. Keeping in mind the advocacy process, advocates should leave the client with a clear understanding of what will happen next.

2.6.4: Dealing with hostility

As stated in the previous chapter the majority of complaint handlers and professionals recognise the benefits of advocacy support to their clients. However, in a minority of cases, advocates may encounter open hostility when progressing a client's complaint. This hostility can be in the form of aggressive, discriminatory or abusive language or behaviour, or a questioning of the advocate's professionalism. In these circumstances, it is important that the advocate recognises these behaviours and knows when and how to report problems and seek support; this is particularly important for less-experienced advocates. Advocates working for professional organisations will have access to supervision and support in these circumstances. However, peer advocates who are volunteers may not be well supported.

In all circumstances, it is important for the advocate to try to record, as soon as possible, the details of any incidences of open hostility, including what (if anything was said), any non-verbal gestures, the time and place, and details of any witnesses. This is useful for self-reflection if a pattern of hostility emerges but is also useful if the matter needs to be escalated, or if the advocate themselves receive a counter-allegation. Advocates should write these records as close in time to the incident as possible and should mark the date and time of the record.

Sometimes the advocate may feel they are able to overlook minor, one-off instances of hostility. For most occasions, after a short period for reflection and objectivity, it may be appropriate for the advocate to discuss the perceived hostility informally with the person either face-to-face or over the phone. It is always possible that the advocate has misunderstood or misinterpreted the actions of another professional or that the advocate has made a mistake. Raising the issue as soon as possible is important. Advocates should keep conciliation at the forefront of their mind; the purpose of any such conversation is to be able to move forward with the complaint, not to prove who was right or wrong. Again, detailed records should be kept.

Where such an informal conversation is not possible, or where it has not been successful, professional advocates may wish to ask for their manager to contact the institution. Volunteer advocates may wish to raise the matter to management themselves. Advocates themselves of course have the right to complain about institutions in their own right, particularly where they have been subject to aggressive, discriminatory or abusive behaviour by an officer of that institution.

The advocate should also consider whether they need to inform their client about the situation. Some organisations will have policies about this. The advocate will have to judge between the need for transparency in the advocacy relationship and the client's ongoing relationship with that institution. The client may wish to have the option to change to another advocate if the advocate's relationship with the organisation is likely to obstruct the client's complaint.

Clients may also be hostile to their advocates. Professional advocates should follow their organisations policies with regards to managing risk and abusive behaviour (See Chapter 1). Informal advocates can take general precautions and reassert expectations and boundaries to the client, perhaps going over the initial advocacy agreement. However, if an advocate feels at risk from the client and interventions have not improved the situation then the advocate has the right to discontinue the advocacy relationship at their discretion.

2.7: Requesting records

It is hoped that in the majority of cases, clients' grievances can be resolved through a straightforward process of liaising with the institution and through the standard complaints process. Occasionally, for complex or historic complaints, the advocate may need to help the client seek access to their records in order to provide evidence for the complaint, or even to ascertain whether there are indeed any grounds for complaint. Section 7 of the Data Protection Act (1998)

However, complainants should not be afraid of making complaints just because they are not clear-cut. Most complaints will be considered on what is known as 'the balance of probabilities'. This refers to the standard of proof that must be reached for a decision to be upheld or not upheld. Most people are familiar with the criminal standard of proof; for the suspect to be guilty in a criminal case, the crime must be proved 'beyond a reasonable doubt'. The balance of probabilities quite simply means that, considering all the available evidence, something is more likely to have occurred than not. For those who prefer statistics, it means that there must be at least a 51 percent likelihood that the thing complained about actually took place. It is useful for advocates to consider this when helping their client identify the specific complaints. If the complaint handler is unlikely to be able to get the facts, it is probable that the complainant will have a decision of 'no finding'.

Even this shouldn't necessarily put complainants off. The issues related to their complaint are nearly always recorded somewhere and can be used to tip the balance of probabilities for the next person who makes a complaint about the same thing. This is particularly true of 'he-said, she-said' complaints. Complaints like these serve to flag up areas of concern to institutions and are important.

Complaints can also result in a 'no finding' where the client's rights are vague. For example, where a law leaves a lot of room for interpretation or where the complainant is complaining about general poor practice. In these cases, it is good for the advocate to help the complainant consider what specifically has given rise to the expectation that something should have been done differently. Perhaps the complainant knows that there is a better policy in a different local authority, perhaps the complainant knows that somebody else in the same position was treated differently, perhaps there exists some non-legally-binding charters or standards or guidance which have not been considered by the institution. Any of these considerations should be included in the complaint.

2.9: Recognising the limits of the complaints procedure

Advocates should be able to recognise when the complaints procedure is not the only option open to the client, by which they could pursue their grievance. In some cases the client may wish to consider raising their grievance to the relevant Ombudsman, pursuing civil compensation or seeking a judicial review. Solicitors and Ombudsmen will often provide helpful advice about the help they can offer. As always, the advocate's task will be to provide information about these options and to help the client weigh up the pros and cons before a decision is made. The advocate should not advise the client to take a particular option. We will discuss these options further in the next chapter.

2.10: Key points

- Detailed referrals and thorough planning for the first meeting will get the advocacy relationship off to a good start.
- Always keep in mind the advocacy process: build trust, gather information, provide information and agree the next steps.
- Complaints should be written, formal and clear.
- Advocates must ensure the complaint being submitted is what the client wants to say.
- Advocacy doesn't end with submitting the complaint.
- Complaints can have different outcomes and the wording of the response needs to be understood and checked by the advocate for accuracy at each stage of the complaint.

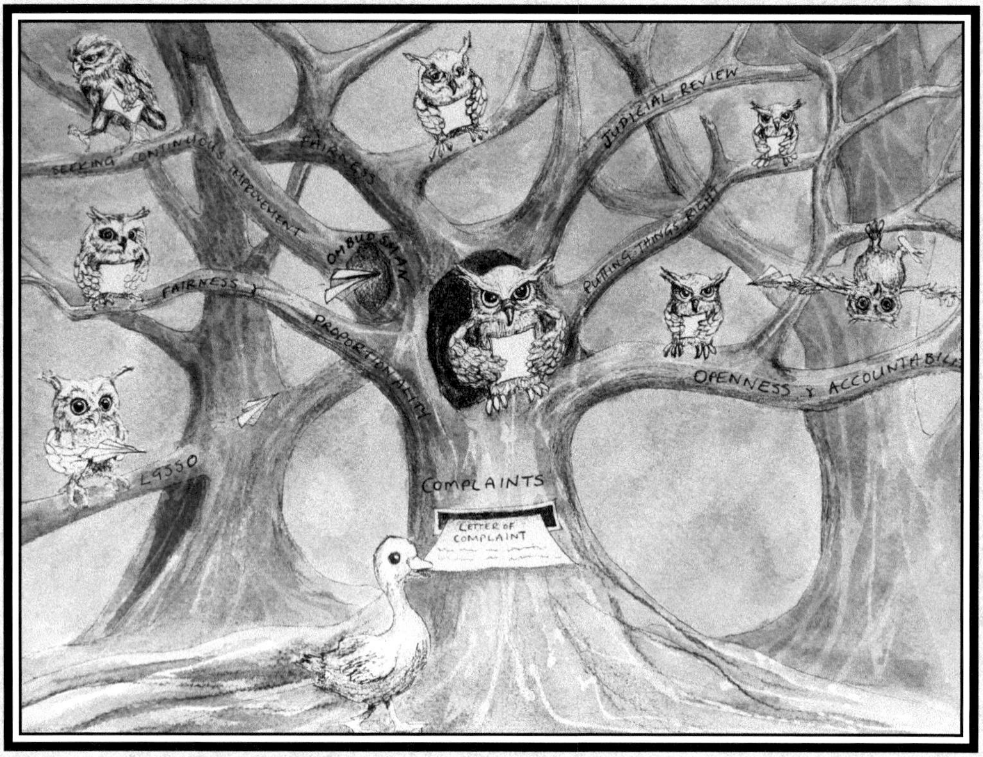

Chapter 3: Understanding the complaints system

3.1: How are complaints systems set up?

Complaining is something we all do, particularly when it comes to public services, many of which are now delivered by charities and companies. It was recognised some time ago by the government that there had to be an effective system whereby ordinary people could complain about a public authority, without having to use lawyers or deal with complex procedures.

The majority of the complaints system in England has a legal basis. If there is no legal basis for the complaints system, then people do not know what their rights are, and they can't enforce them against public institutions. The government builds this legal basis by making acts of parliament (also known as statutes) as well as regulations (also known as statutory instruments). We call these acts and regulations 'legislation.'

In this book, we do not cover complaints systems in Wales, Scotland and Northern Ireland, which are the other parts of the United Kingdom. This is because the law in these countries (or 'jurisdictions' as lawyers call them) is different from that of England.

Different acts and regulations apply to different types of complaint systems. Most public institutions are required to have a complaints system, which has to follow the acts and the regulations, and be accessible to complainants. Each of these systems is addressed in the following chapters. The regulations are like a manual for institutions on how to build and apply a complaints procedure. Regulations are often accompanied by guidance which helps people understand them better. They can be very useful if not essential for advocates.

In this book, when we refer to 'sections' in an Act of Parliament, we use the letter 'S' and then the section number for short.

> An Act of Parliament or a statute is one of the highest forms of law in England. It sets out the basic law of the land, which judges then interpret and apply in individual cases with which they deal.

> Regulations or statutory instruments are not made by parliament but by government departments. They flow from acts of parliament and they implement the intention of the act. They may also be accompanied by guidance that is published alongside the act by a government department.

> Guidance is sometimes published alongside an act. So for instance the Independent Office for Police Conduct Statutory Guidance is issued under Section 22 of the Police Reform Act (2002). Alternatively, guidance may be published by a government department to help people understand an act or regulations

The legal basis or legislation behind complaints procedures are important because they create legal rights for people who use them. Although institutions are not allowed to deviate from these laws, regrettably they sometimes do which is why it is important for advocates to be aware of the legal basis behind the complaints system. Institutions may well need to be reminded of their legal duties.

Moreover, the acts of parliament, regulations and guidance set out the kind of complaints that can be made to institutions. Some complaints will fall outside the complaints system, and it is important to know that at the outset of the complaint.

These acts of parliament and regulations can be found on the government's website at: www.opsi.gov.uk. However, caution should be exercised with the information on this website because the statutes and statutory regulations on this website are not always up-to-date, and statutory laws are often subject to amendment. The editorial team to the www.opsi.gov.uk website do give a warning about 'changes to legislation' and it is possible to see those changes by using their drop-down boxes.

Guidance can be issued following from an act of parliament or it can be published by a government department on its website. This guidance can be extremely helpful to advocates as it explains the basic law and how it is supposed to work in practice. Strictly speaking however, it is not the law. Advocates should nonetheless acquaint themselves with the relevant guidance and read it whenever possible. When we refer to guidance in this book, we will provide an internet link for advocates to find it.

Other institutions, such as local authorities, also publish their own guidance. Again, this guidance can be very helpful but it may not reflect the precise law contained in acts of parliament, regulations or government guidance.

In each of the chapters in this book we set out some of the legislation which is applicable to a complaints process and which can be referenced in an advocate's complaint. What we have tried to do is summarise very briefly what that legislation says. Regrettably, this is no substitute for reading the legislation itself. In practical terms, we realise that very few advocates will have the time and the resources to tackle legislation which can be extremely complex. Nonetheless, referencing the legal basis for your client's right to complain may make the difference between acceptance and refusal of the complaint.

We have tried to keep legal references as straightforward as possible in this book. However, advocates will still need to pay careful attention to make sure that they understand the different pieces of legislation and how they fit together to create a comprehensive complaints system.

As an example, S26 of the Children Act (1989) says that there must be a proper complaints system in place. However, it is the Children Act (1989) Representations Procedure (England) Regulations 2006, which describes how that complaints system actually works. So, an advocate might state at the start of a complaint that they are bringing that complaint under S26 of the 1989 act and the 2006 regulations.

One more thing – when we refer to an act of parliament such as the Children Act 1989 or regulations such as the Children Act 1989 Representations Procedure (England) Regulations 2006, we call them for short 'the 1989 act' or the '2006 regulations'.

3.2: Different institutions working together

Advocates need to be aware that many public services are delivered by a variety of institutions, both public and private. These institutions include charities, private companies and even individuals. One example would be a local authority and a private company providing care to an individual. Another would be two local authorities caring for a child, one with a care order over the child and the other who provides a foster carer. Generally, complaints systems oblige institutions to work together and cooperate to resolve complaints. It is important in this kind of situation to identify which institution is responsible for whatever has gone wrong. Very often it can be extremely helpful to look at which institution is under a legal obligation to care for or provide support to that complainant. It is not unknown for institutions to try and pass responsibility for a problem between themselves, which can lead to delay in resolving a complaint.

It can be helpful in this kind of situation to seek advice from the Ombudsman or one of the institutions which oversee a complaints system such as the Independent Office for Police Conduct (whom we will discuss in Chapter 10). Alternatively, advocates can seek advice from a lawyer.

3.3: Maladministration

Complaints are all about 'maladministration'. Maladministration means – in brief terms – 'getting it wrong'.

The Parliamentary and Health Services Ombudsman has published guidance, which can be found at: www.ombudsman.org.uk/about-us/our-principles/principles-good-complaint-handling

This guidance says that 'good administration' by public bodies means:

- **Getting it right** – a public body must follow the law and its own policy/guidance.
- **Being customer focused** – a public body needs to focus on the needs of the service user and avoid delay in delivering its services.
- **Being open and accountable** – a public body needs to provide accurate information and avoid giving misleading information.
- **Acting fairly and proportionately** – public bodies need to make reasoned decisions and act on the correct information. They cannot discriminate unlawfully against a person or act in an arbitrary or unfair way. There must be no bias or conflict of interest on their part when a decision is taken.
- **Putting things right** – the public body should apologise to the complainant and take steps to remedy the situation.
- **Seeking continuous improvement** – public bodies need to be self-critical. They must learn from their mistakes.

A local authority has the power to award compensation in cases of maladministration under S92 of the Local Government Act (2000).

3.4: How the complaints system works

A complaint typically begins with a letter or a written representation made to an institution. Generally speaking, the institute investigates the complaint and then responds. Then, depending on the nature of the complaint, the complainant may have the right to take the matter further and have the complaint looked at again. Institutions generally operate two or three stages of complaint. If the complainant is satisfied at any stage, that is the end of the complaints procedure.

3.5: The role of the Ombudsman and other similar institutions

The majority of complaints systems have an appeal process – that is to say the complainant can go to a higher body to get the complaint reviewed or looked at again. Local authorities and some public institutions have Ombudsmen to review their complaints. These Ombudsmen are set up under an act of parliament. Likewise, other reviewing organisations, such as the Independent Office for Police Conduct have a similar legal basis.

The concept of the Ombudsman covers both the public and the private sector. Ombudsman Services is a private organisation that provides an Ombudsman to a wide range of industries such as energy and communications.

There is also the Ombudsman Association, which includes public sector Ombudsmen, such as the Local Government and Social Care Ombudsman as well as private sector Ombudsmen, such as Ombudsman Services. Their website can be found at: www.ombudsmanassociation.org.

In this chapter, we look briefly at the role of the Local Government and Social Care Ombudsman, which deals with complaints about local authorities and social services. We also look at the Parliamentary and Health Services Ombudsman, which deals with complaints about government departments and the National Health Service. Other Ombudsmen and their roles are covered in later chapters.

In Chapters 4 and 5 we deal with social care for children and adults. The organisation that oversees the complaints system here is the Local Government and Social Care Ombudsman. We consider how that Ombudsman works in this chapter.

In Chapter 6 we deal with the healthcare complaints system, which is subject to the Parliamentary and Health Service Ombudsman.

In Chapter 7 we deal with education complaints, which is subject to the Department for Education and other government bodies.

In Chapter 8 we deal with housing issues, which are subject to the Housing Ombudsman.

In Chapter 9 we deal with complaints about benefits, which are subject to the Parliamentary and Health Services Ombudsman.

In Chapter 10 we deal with complaints about the police which are subject to the Independent Office for Police Conduct and the Crown Prosecution Service, which is subject to the Independent Assessor of Complaints.

In Chapter 11 we deal with complaints about utility and other private companies.

In Chapter 12 we deal with complaints about data protection where the overseeing organisation is the Information Commissioner.

In Chapter 13 we deal with complaints about lawyers which are subject to the Legal Ombudsman.

In Chapter 14 we deal with complaints about the Prison and Probation Service which is dealt with by the Prisons and Probation Ombudsman.

3.6: The Local Government and Social Care Ombudsman (LGSCO)

Where a complainant is dissatisfied with a local authority's complaints procedure he can submit a complaint to the LGSCO.

3.6.1: The statutory basis for the LGSCO

Part III of the Local Government Act (1974) set up the LGSCO, otherwise known as the Commissioner for Local Administration. S24A of the 1974 act says that the LGSCO can investigate local authorities in relation to complaints made by members of the public, who claim to have sustained injustice in consequence of maladministration.

3.6.2: Who can complain to the LGSCO?

The LGSCO cannot investigate a complaint unless it has been submitted first of all to the local authority. The complaint can be submitted to the LGSCO by the complainant, or by a person on his behalf, or by a member of the local authority (which means a local councillor). The LGSCO can actually launch an investigation, if someone within the local authority has been asked to refer the complaint to them but has not done so. S27(1) says that either an individual, or body of persons incorporated or not (i.e. a charity), can complain to the LGSCO. A complaint may also be brought by the representatives of a deceased person.

3.6.3: What the LGSCO cannot investigate

S26(6) then says that the LGSCO cannot investigate:

- any action where there is a right of appeal, reference or review to a tribunal
- any action where there is a right of appeal to a government department
- any action where the complainant has or had the right to sue the public body in a court of law.

In addition, under Schedule 5 to the 1974 act, the LGSCO cannot investigate the following matters:

- The commencement or conduct of civil or criminal proceedings before any court of law (which includes a tribunal).
- Action taken by any police authority in connection with the investigation or prevention of crime.

So, in short, where there are other legal proceedings going on at the same time as the complaint, or there is a clear right to sue a local authority, then the LGSCO will probably decline to accept the complaint.

Schedule 5 also excludes other types of local authority activity, such as activity connected with its status as a registered provider of social housing (See Chapter 8).

3.6.4: Time limits

There is a time limit for going to the LGSCO. S26B of the 1974 act says that the application must be made in writing and 'before the end of the permitted period'.

3.6.6: What can the LGSCO do by way of remedying a complaint?

The LGSCO can recommend various remedies to the institution concerned. These will be practical in nature and may include an apology, the offer of mediation between the complainant and the local authority, financial compensation, or a recommendation to reinstate or implement a support package.

The LGSCO publishes its own *Guidance on Good Practice: Remedies*. The latest version can be found at: www.lgo.org.uk/assets/attach/2619/Remedies-V4-FINAL-12.1.2016.pdf

The guidance is something that anyone making or dealing with a complaint should read. It deals with many different types of complaints and spells out how the LGSCO will deal with those complaints, and the remedies that they are likely to recommend.

However it is important to realise that the LGSCO cannot:

- Enforce a remedy which they have recommended.
- Substitute their decision for one taken properly by a body in their jurisdiction.
- Recommend disciplinary action against staff.
- Award compensation, punitive damages or costs in the same way as a court or tribunal would do.
- Calculate a financial remedy based on what the cost of the service would have been to the provider.
- Be bound by precedent. This means that if they make a previous decision on a matter, they do not have to follow that decision in another similar matter.
- Be a substitute for any statutory appeal process.

In their guidance on remedies, the LGSCO says that complainants should not need lawyers to help them make a complaint to the LGSCO. As a consequence, legal fees are not payable unless the circumstances are exceptional, for instance if the case is very complex. In those circumstances, they may make a contribution rather than pay the whole bill.

3.6.7: Information about the LGSCO

The LGSCO's website can be found at: www.lgo.org.uk. The website has a facility for searching decisions at: http://www.lgo.org.uk/decisions. The LGSCO also has a database of decision categories:

- Adult care services.
- Children's services.
- Benefits and tax.
- Education.
- Environment and regulation.
- Housing.
- Transport and highways.
- Planning.
- Health.
- Other services – land, leisure and culture, elections and councillor conduct.

There is also the investigation manual for the Local Government and Social Care Ombudsman. This describes in detail the internal workings of the Ombudsman's office, and how they pursue investigations. This can be found at: www.lgo.org.uk/information-centre/staff-guidance/investigation-manual.

3.7: The Draft Public Service Ombudsman Act

This act, when it is brought into force, will merge the LGSCO and the Parliamentary and Health Service Ombudsman (PHSO) and bring them into one office, the Public Service Ombudsman (PSO). The framework of the act is also intended to bring other jurisdictions within the PSO in time. S26 of the act allows the government to make further legislation to bring the Housing Ombudsman into the remit of the PSO in the future.

Both the LGSCO and the PHSO welcome the new act. They believe that one complaints Ombudsman will make it easier for people to complain when they have been let down by a public service. The act will not change the basic way in which the Ombudsman's system works. It will still act as a final tier above the basic complaints procedures, which are operated by public institutions and certain private organisations providing public services.

However, the new PSO can widen the scope of an investigation where it is satisfied that the injustice suffered as a result of any maladministration goes beyond an individual. The PSO is also given greater powers to share information with others, who have oversight of particular services and where there may be a threat to public health and safety.

3.8: Other legal routes

There are various ways of bringing legal action through the courts against public institutions. One of the most commonly seen methods of legal action is judicial review, which we explain below. Another is a claim for compensation against a public institution, for something that it has done or should not have done.

As we advised in Chapter 1, this is a situation where seeking the advice of a law firm is particularly important. Clients will often say to an advocate that they want to 'sue' a public institution and take them to court. As we explained in Chapter 1, it is very useful to be able to explain the limits of what the advocate can do for them, and what a law firm might be able to achieve. Advocates will not be able to give a detailed explanation as to whether a certain course of legal action is appropriate. However, being aware of the existence of other legal options will help manage their client's legal expectations.

It is also important to realise that in certain circumstances, for instance with a complaint brought on behalf of a child, bringing legal action through the court may mean the end of the complaints process. We consider this issue in more detail in later chapters.

In the writers' experience, it is actually very difficult indeed to take this kind of legal action forward without some kind of financial funding/legal aid. In practice, it can be very hard to get a case off the ground. Moreover, clients often think that instructing a solicitor means that they will 'get their day in court'. In reality, the vast majority of legal disputes, particularly in the examples set out on the next page, are settled out of court.

At the same time, there are a number of tribunals that exist for the resolution of disputes in relation to various matters, including entitlement to state and local authority benefits, health, education and social care and inclusion on the Disclosure and Barring Service. A list of these courts and tribunals and what they do, can be found at: www.gov.uk/government/organisations/hm-courts-and-tribunals-service/about#our-tribunals.

The following are just some of the legal areas where courts and tribunals will be involved and specialist legal knowledge will be needed.

3.8.1: Judicial review

Judicial review is a way of challenging a public institution's decision through the courts. As a general rule, judicial review is concerned with present and future actions and does not look into historic issues. There are very strict time limits for commencing judicial review proceedings, which can only be exceeded with the permission of the court. Judicial review rarely involves the award of any kind of compensation.

Judicial review is normally only available after all other forms of internal appeal within a local authority have been exhausted. It relates to the local authority's decision in respect of a particular issue. For example, if an initial decision is made and this was to be challenged internally by way of review/appeal, it would be the final decision on review or appeal that would be the subject matter of the judicial review.

The process of judicial review generally requires the help of a law firm. It may begin with what is known as a 'letter of claim' (it may be alternatively called a 'letter before claim' or 'pre-action letter'); this is a letter written by a lawyer setting out the action/omission/decision being challenged, the law, and the remedy that is being sought. Letter of claims must receive a response within a deadline, usually 14 days, though it can be less if there are good reasons for this. If the situation is not sufficiently resolved by the deadline, then the case progresses to the issue of proceedings and potentially, a court hearing. There are very restrictive time limits that apply in judicial review claims.

Normally a person undertaking judicial review will have solicitors with whom they can discuss these issues. A court dealing with a judicial review application can make a legal costs order in favour of the person applying, and legal aid may also be available in very limited circumstances. It is also possible for the court to make a legal costs order against the person who issues the proceedings for judicial review if they were unsuccessful. These costs could be substantial.

As stated, there are very tight time limits for judicial review proceedings, which are beyond the scope of this book. It is essential to consult a lawyer who has expertise in this particular area as soon as possible.

3.8.2: Children Act proceedings and children in care generally

It may be possible for children (that is, people under the age of 18) to apply to a family court under the Children Act (1989). A 'looked after child' (a child subject to a care order) might typically seek permission to apply to court and if permission is granted, apply to court in connection with contact with their parent or siblings. They may only have indirect contact and they want direct contact or perhaps, following a looked after child (LAC) review, contact may be reviewed or terminated. It would be more typical for parents to make such an application but applications by children do occur. Legal aid would be required for this application via a solicitor specialising in Children Act proceedings and is not easy to obtain.

If a looked after child was, for example, about to be removed from a foster placement into a residential placement, or there was an important issue relating to education or medical treatment, then the child might seek the advice of a solicitor specialising in Children Act proceedings with a view to using the process of judicial review to challenge the decision of a local authority in a court. Again, legal aid would be required and would be difficult to obtain in these circumstances.

3.8.3: State benefits

There are legal procedures to challenge an award or refusal of benefits. There is a specific type of court, the First-tier Tribunal (social security and child support), which is responsible for handling appeals against decisions relating to a range of benefits, including carer's allowance, child benefit, child support, employment support allowance, disability living allowance, personal independent payments, income support and jobseeker's allowance.

3.8.4: Care standards

Organisations and individuals that provide care to adults and children have to meet minimum standards, and have their staff properly vetted. There is a specific type of court, the First-tier Tribunal (Care Standards), which is responsible for handling appeals against decisions by the Secretary of State for Education, the Secretary of State for Health, the Care Quality Commission and Ofsted that exclude, remove or suspend a person or an organisation from a register to work with or care for children or vulnerable adults.

Care standards are important, particularly where a child or an adult has been placed in an institution that is failing. A complaint made to one of the bodies mentioned on the previous page, can have the effect of persuading the body complained to, to initiate proceedings to have that institution closed or at the very least investigated.

3.8.5: Mental health

A person who is admitted (whether on a voluntary or compulsory basis) to a psychiatric hospital may have the right to ask to be discharged. There is a specific type of court, the First-tier Tribunal (Mental Health), which is responsible for handling applications for the discharge of patients detained in psychiatric hospitals.

3.8.6: Special educational needs

Many children have special educational needs, for which they receive support from the local authority. There is a type of specific court, called the First-tier Tribunal (special educational needs and disability), which exists to handle appeals against local authority decisions regarding special educational needs, including a refusal to:

- assess a child's educational, health and care (EHC) needs
- make a statement of their special educational needs
- reassess their special educational needs
- create an EHC plan
- change what's in a child's special educational needs statement or EHC plan
- maintain the statement or EHC plan.

3.8.7: Personal injury claims

As we saw in the previous section, judicial review is a way of challenging decisions made by public institutions through the courts. Personal injury claims are claims for compensation for injuries suffered by the complainant and which are brought through the courts. The following are examples:

- Negligence on the part of a public institution for failure to protect the complainant from harm or neglect – for example a person who suffers injury as a result of a medical mistake or a child who has been abused as a result of the local authority failing to take them into care.

- A direct claim against someone in the employment of the public institution who has harmed the complainant, for instance a police officer, a teacher or a care worker.

As with judicial review, this is a claim that requires the expert advice of a qualified lawyer. The claim is normally begun with a letter of claim, and then it can progress to the issue of court proceedings, which in very rare circumstances leads to a trial. The vast majority of compensation claims are settled out of court.

There are strict time limits for bringing civil actions for compensation – again this is beyond the scope of this book. Normally such claims are brought under 'no win no fee' arrangements. However, they can be very expensive for lawyers to take on and consequently they may not be viable.

3.8.8: The Criminal Injuries Compensation Authority

Advocates work with children and vulnerable people who may have been victims of abuse. The Criminal Injuries Compensation Authority (CICA) is a government organisation that compensates victims of 'crimes of violence'.

It is quite separate from the system for judicial review and personal injury claims but it represents an alternative way of getting compensation. Some local authorities help children in care make claims to the CICA.

The compensation that the CICA award is partly based on is a 'tariff system' and may be less than what a victim of abuse recovers in a personal injury claim. On the other hand, the CICA may be the only possible source of compensation for instance, where a personal injury claim against an institution or an individual is unlikely to succeed. The terms of the present CICA Scheme can be found at: www.gov.uk/government/organisations/criminal-injuries-compensation-authority/about#who-we-are.

It can be very difficult to find a lawyer to handle a CICA claim. This is because generally speaking, the lawyer's costs have to come out of the CICA award, and the awards can be very low. Advocates should check with their organisation as to whether helping a client with a CICA claim is part of their role.

3.9: Key points

- The majority of complaints systems in England have a legal basis.
- Their legal basis can be found in acts of parliament, regulations and guidance.
- Sometimes a complaint can be against more than one institution; generally institutions are obliged to work together.
- Complaints are about 'maladministration', which basically means 'getting it wrong'. Local authorities can award compensation for maladministration.
- Ombudsmen are independent and impartial institutions that may be able to help the complainant.
- Advocates should be aware that there may be other legal routes open to complainants such as: judicial review, Children Act proceedings, special tribunals, personal injury claims and compensation from the Criminal Injuries Compensation Authority.

GUIDANCE
SUPPORT
REASSURANCE
THE TASK OF THE ADVOCATE
CHILDREN ACT 2004
JUSTICE
DUTY OF CARE
CARE
HOPE

Chapter 4: Complaints about children's services

4.1: Introduction

This chapter concerns children's social services. Advocates need to be aware that the law distinguishes between different types of children. First of all, there are children in care – looked after children, secondly there are children who require support, whom we call children in need, and finally we have care leavers, who are leaving the care system. Complaints can be brought by these children or their parents, or their representatives. The Children Act (1989) set up a complaints system under which a child could make a complaint to the local authority.

4.2: The complaints system for children's services

S26 of the Children Act 1989 required the state to set up a system of complaints handling for children. In addition, the Children (Leaving Care) Act (2000) inserted S24D into the Children Act (1989) so as to set up a complaints system for children leaving the care system. This complaints system was later extended to adoption by the Adoption and Children Act (2002) and to guardianship by the Health and Social Care (Community Health and Standards) Act (2003).

S26(3) of the 1989 act says that every local authority has to establish a procedure for considering any representations (including any complaint) made to them by the following people:

- Any child who is being looked after by them or who is not being looked after by them but is in need.
- A parent.
- Any person who is not a parent but who has parental responsibility for them.
- Any local authority foster parent.

- Such other person as the authority consider has a sufficient interest in the child's welfare to warrant the child's representations being considered by them.

A person can complain about the local authority's 'qualifying functions' which are:

- The provision of services for children and their families.
- The provision of accommodation for children.
- The duties of local authorities in relation to children looked after by them.
- Visiting.
- Advice and assistance for certain children and young persons.
- Personal advisers and pathway plans.
- Secure accommodation.
- Independent reviewing officers.
- Care and supervision orders.
- The effect of care orders.
- Parental contact.
- Child assessment orders.
- The emergency protection of children.

In addition, the complaints procedure covers the following adoption functions:

- The provision of adoption support services.
- The placement of children by an adoption agency for adoption.
- The removal of children who are or may be placed by adoption agencies.
- The removal of children in non-adoption agency cases.
- The duties of an adoption agency considering adoption and the proposed placement of a child with a prospective adopter.
- Placement and reviews.
- Case records.
- Foreign adoption.

The complaints procedure also covers specified guardianship functions.

S24D(1) of the 1989 act says that each local authority has to establish a complaints procedure for care leavers.

Care leavers are, very briefly, children who were looked after by a local authority but who are entitled to further local authority support under the 1989 act after the age of sixteen, and in some cases up to the age of 25. The precise definition of a care leaver and their entitlement to support is a complex subject and beyond the scope of this book. Certain charities publish very helpful guidance – for instance Coram Voice: http://www.coramvoice.org.uk/young-peoples-zone/are-you-care-leaver.

4.3: The duty to appoint an advocate

S26A of the Children Act (1989) imposes a duty on local authorities to provide advocacy services for children in care, children in need and care leavers, who are making complaints under the Children Act (1989) representations procedure.

The relevant regulations are the Advocacy Services and Representations Procedure (Children) (Amendment) Regulations (2004).

Regulation 3 says that an advocate cannot act for a child in making a complaint if:

- they are the subject of the complaint
- they are responsible for the management of a person who is the subject of the complaint
- they manage the services which is or may be the subject of the complaint
- they have control over the resources allocated to the service which is or may the subject of the complaint
- they are or may become involved in the consideration of the representation on behalf of the local authority.

Under Regulation 4, where a local authority becomes aware that a person or child intends to make a complaint, they must provide the person or child with information about advocacy services and offer them help in obtaining an advocate.

Under Regulation 5 a local authority must monitor the steps that they have taken with a view to ensuring that they comply with these regulations, in particular by keeping a record about each advocate appointed under arrangements made by the local authority.

4.4: The Children Act (1989) Representations Procedure (England) Regulations (2006)

The statutory legislation uses the word 'complaint' and 'representation'. The regulations say that 'complainant' means a person making representations. In this chapter, we use both words interchangeably.

4.4.1: Guidance

Advocates are referred to the guidance *Getting the Best from Complaints* published by the Department for Education and Skills. This document refers to the 2006 regulations and provides a very helpful guide to the procedure to be followed by local authorities dealing with children's and care leavers' complaints. It can be found at: www.gov.uk/government/publications/childrens-social-care-getting-the-best-from-complaints.

4.4.2: The main stages

The 2006 Regulations set out the procedure, which is in three stages:

- Stage 1: local resolution.
- Stage 2: investigation.
- Stage 3: review panel.

4.4.3: What complaints can be considered

Regulation 6 states that any complaint may be made orally or in writing and under Regulation 7 may be withdrawn in the same way. Regulation 8 sets out those complaints that cannot be considered. These are complaints where:

- The complainant has stated in writing to the local authority that he is taking, or intends to take, proceedings in any court or tribunal – for instance a compensation claim against the local authority.
- The local authority is taking or proposing to take disciplinary proceedings against any person – this could be for instance, against a social worker involved with a child.
- The local authority has been notified that any person is conducting an investigation in contemplation of criminal proceedings, or where criminal

proceedings are pending – for instance the prosecution of someone who is looking after the child.

In each of the above cases, the local authority must have decided that consideration, or further consideration, of the complaint would prejudice the conduct of any proceedings or investigation.

If they do so, then they must notify the complainant in writing, and if any of the circumstances that are preventing a complaint being made are discontinued or completed, then the complainant may resubmit their complaint. They must do so no later than one year after the discontinuance or completion of the circumstances that held up the complaint in the first place.

As we saw in Chapter 3, mistakes made by local authorities in relation to children and adults can sometimes form the subject of compensation claims, which are brought through the civil courts. These can prove very expensive, not least because the award of compensation is accompanied by legal costs (which can be as much as, if not more than, the actual compensation amount). On the other hand, a complaint may cost the local authority very much less. There are situations where the complaints process is in fact the best way forward because it is quicker and less costly for the complainant. At the end of this chapter, we set out some examples of those cases that have been put before the Local Government and Social Care Ombudsman and it can be seen that some of the recommended compensation awards are quite high.

This is one of those matters on which advice should be taken by a solicitor specialising in compensation claims brought against social services by children.

It is important to bear in mind what we saw in Chapter 3 about the limits to the remit of the Local Government and Social Care Ombudsman. According to S26(6) and Schedule 5 of the Local Government Act (1974), the LGSCO cannot investigate issues where there are other legal processes available.

4.4.4: Time limits

Regulation 9 contains the time limits for making a complaint. Briefly, a complainant must make their representations about a matter no later than one year after the grounds to make the representations arose. This time limit can be waived by a local authority if, having regard to all the circumstances, they conclude that it would not be reasonable to expect the complainant to have made the representations within the time limit; and notwithstanding the time that has it as necessary. That written record then becomes the complaint. Regulation 16 underlines how important it is for any person making a complaint to set out the issues in the complaint clearly. A child or care leaver may have great difficulty doing that, or putting those issues onto paper without the support of an adult.

- Stage 1 should be completed within 10 working days from when the complaint was submitted orally or in writing.
- The deadline can be extended to 20 working days if agreed or if the complaint is complex.

4.4.10: Stage 2: investigation

Regulation 17 sets out the next stage following the local resolution procedure in Regulation 14. In practice, Stage 2 complaints will be investigated by what is known as an investigating officer.

The regulations do not contain any mention of an investigating officer, but their role is set out in *Getting the Best from Complaints* (see p.78).

The investigating officer may be appointed from inside or outside the local authority however they must be sufficiently independent from the staff, team or service complained about. So, for example, if a complainant made a complaint about an adoption service, a senior manager from a care-leaving service could be the investigating officer.

Regulation 17 provides for the appointment of an 'Independent Person'. Their role is to make sure the process is open and transparent and that the young person stays the focus of all the professionals involved in resolving the complaint. They typically shadow the investigating officer in meetings, discussions and reviews of documents but their role is not a passive one and they are able to intervene or make recommendations if they are not satisfied with how the investigation is being pursued.

The local authority must consider the complainant's representations, with the Independent Person, and send notice of their response within 25 working days of the date on which it was agreed not to use local resolution or from the date on which the complainant requested an investigation. This is known as the 'start date'. This date can be extended to 65 working days but, again, this should really only happen where there is a good reason and the complainant must be informed.

The local authority's response to the complaint must include information about the complainant's right, under regulation 18, to request that the representations be further considered by a Stage 3 panel and the procedure for making such a request.

- An independent person must be appointed for a Stage 2 investigation.
- The investigation should be completed with 25 working days.
- An extension to 65 working days can be agreed with the complainant.

4.4.11: Stage 3: review panel

Regulation 18 is the next stage. Where the complainant is dissatisfied with the outcome of the Stage 2 investigation of their complaint, they may request that their complaint be escalated to Stage 3 – a review panel. There is a time limit for making this kind of request. It must be made within 20 working days of receiving the response to the Stage 2 investigation. The request to escalate the complaint must set out the reasons for the complainant's dissatisfaction with the outcome of the investigation.

Regulation 19 sets out the procedure of the review panel stage. Where the local authority has received a suitable request, they must appoint a panel of three independent persons to consider the representations. The panel cannot include the independent person and investigating officer of the Stage 2 investigation. The panel has to meet within 30 working days of the local authority receiving a request for it. At its meeting, it must consider any oral or written submissions made by the complainant, the local authority, and any other person who has a sufficient interest in the proceedings.

The regulations state that the panel must hear any Independent Person appointed for the Stage 2 investigation, if that Independent Person wishes to make representations. The complainant is entitled to have either their advocate, or any other person of their choice, present at the meeting to speak on their behalf.

Following that meeting the panel compiles a written report setting out a brief summary of the complaint and the panel's recommendations. Within 5 working days of the meeting the panel must send its report to the local authority, the complainant and his advocate or representative, the Stage 2 Independent Person and any other person with a sufficient interest. Within 15 working days of receiving the panel's recommendations the local authority must determine how the authority will respond to them and what they propose to do in the light of them. They must also send to the complainant its response and proposals, along with information about making a complaint to the Local Government and Social Care Ombudsman.

- The complainant's request for a Stage 3 review panel must be made within 20 days of receiving the local authority's Stage 2 response.
- The panel must meet within 30 days of receiving the complainant's request.
- The panel report must be produced within 5 working days of the panel meeting.
- The local authority must issue a response within 15 working day of receiving the review panel report.

4.5: Voluntary organisations

Regulations 21 and 22 apply to voluntary organisations that provide accommodation for children. These will be not for profit companies operating accommodation such as children's homes. They are required under S59(4)(b) of the Children Act (1989) to operate the same complaints procedure detailed above for children, a parent, a person with parental responsibility or a person with a sufficient interest.

However, there are differences. First of all, voluntary organisations are not subject to the monitoring requirements set out in Regulation 13. Secondly, Regulation 22(2)(b) states that when voluntary organisations apply the regulations, all references to advocates are omitted, which means that they do not need to refer a complainant to an advocate or advocacy service, or notify a person's advocate of a decision.

Consequently, an advocate acting for a child in private accommodation needs to think carefully as to whether the complaint should be brought to the local authority in addition to the voluntary organisation.

4.6: Children's homes

Regulation 39 of the Children's Homes (England) Regulations (2015) requires a children's home to establish a procedure for considering complaints made by or on behalf of children. This procedure must provide that no person, who is the subject of a complaint, takes any part in its consideration or investigation, except at the informal resolution stage if the registered person considers it appropriate. The registered person must ensure that a record is made of any complaint, the action taken in response, and the outcome of any investigation. Moreover, the registered person must ensure that no child is subject to any reprisal for making a complaint or representation. The children's home must ensure that an independent person visits the children's home at least once each month.

Persons who carry on or manage a children's home must be registered with the Office for Standards in Education, Children's Services and Skills (Ofsted) and so if the complainant is dissatisfied with the home's handling of the complaint, he or she can complain to the Chief Inspector at Ofsted.

The 2015 regulations include the provision of secure accommodation for children. This is a specialist form of accommodation which restricts the child's liberty. Local authorities can use this kind of accommodation, under S25 of the Children Act (1989), as a 'last resort' for children who are likely to suffer significant harm, or injure someone else.

4.7: Independent fostering agencies – The Fostering Services (England) Regulations (2011)

If a child wants to complain about their foster carer, it is important for the advocate to establish whether the carer is a local authority foster carer or whether they are retained by an independent fostering agency.

Independent fostering agencies are required under Regulation 18 of these regulations to establish a written procedure for considering complaints made by or on behalf of children placed by the agency, and by foster parents approved by the agency. The procedure is not very specific, other than to provide for an early informal resolution stage and that the procedure cannot involve someone who is the subject of the complaint. The agency must publish its procedure.

The agency also has to keep a written record of the complaint, ensure that children are enabled to make a complaint or representation and ensure that no child is subject to any reprisal for making a complaint or representation.

Once again, an advocate acting for a child in the care of a private fostering agency needs to think carefully as to whether the complaint should be brought to the local authority in addition to the fostering agency.

Independent fostering agencies fall under Ofsted and so if the complainant is dissatisfied with the agency's handling of the complaint, he or she can complain to the chief inspector at Ofsted. The foster agency is obliged to give the complainant the details of the chief inspector and the procedure for complaining.

Agencies must also, on request, supply the chief inspector at Ofsted with a statement containing a summary of any complaints made during the preceding 12 months and the actions taken in response.

4.8: The role of the Local Government and Social Care Ombudsman (LGSCO)

As we saw in Chapter 3, if a complainant is dissatisfied with the local authority's complaints process, he can take the matter to the Local Government and Social Care Ombudsman, who will decide whether the complaint comes within their remit and investigate it.

In March 2015, the LGSCO published a report *Are we Getting the Best from Children's Social Care Complaints?* http://www.lgo.org.uk/information-centre/reports/focus-reports.

The report came to the following conclusions:

- Only a small proportion of complaints came from young people or those acting on their behalf. Most came from parents, family or friends.
- The system could become process driven rather than outcome focused. In other words, following the process became more important than finding a satisfactory outcome.
- The system did not allow the local authority to exercise its judgment about curtailing the three-stage process when it was apparent that resolution would not be likely.
- Some local authorities were finding it difficult to find suitably qualified Independent Persons.
- There was a question mark over whether the third stage – the independent review panel – added anything, when it was unlikely to significantly affect the outcome.

At the same time, the LGSCO identified delays in the system, failure by local authorities to recognise a complaint, a refusal to go through all the statutory stages and failures to choose the correct procedures.

4.9: Key points

- The Children Act (1989) set up a complaints system under which a child could make a complaint to the local authority. That system was extended to care leavers, adopted children and children under guardianship.

- The Adoption and Children Act (2002) imposes a duty on local authorities to provide advocacy services for children in care, children in need and care leavers.

- The complaint system is ultimately subject to the Local Government and Social Care Ombudsman.

- The 1989 act says that every local authority has to establish a complaints procedure for children and care leavers.

- *Getting the Best from Complaints* is an invaluable guide to the system, published by the Department for Education and Skills.

- There are three stages to the complaints procedure: local resolution, independent investigation and panel review.

- A complainant must make their representations within one year.

- Once the local authority has the complaint, it has to provide the complainant with details of its procedure and information about advocacy services.

- Children's homes and independent fostering agencies have different rules.

4.10: Case studies from the LGSCO

The LGSCO's website has a facility for searching decisions: http://www.lgo.org.uk/decisions. We now consider a number of complaints, which have gone before the Ombudsman. It is important to realise that the remedies recommended by the Ombudsman are not restricted to compensation but also include remedies such as an apology or reinstatement of services. Not all of these complaints appear on the LGSCO's website. For each report we have provided the website page.

A website has been set up in conjunction with the writing of this book, to assist advocates work out the kind of remedies that are appropriate for a particular complaint. This can be found at: http://www.complaintadvocates.co.uk/.

Children in need

Respite care and transparency of panel decision

http://www.lgo.org.uk/decisions/children-s-care-services/disabled-children/14-010-195

Miss X complained about the council's decision that she did not qualify for short-breaks assistance for her young son Y, who is disabled. The decision was made by a panel but the notes from the panel only showed who attended not how the panel reached its decision. She also complained that the council had delayed in carrying out a carer's assessment of her. As a result she said she could not spend time alone with her older child and she could not socialise. She said Y was missing opportunities to make friends and to increase his independence.

The Ombudsman recommended the council retake its decision on respite and carry out a new carer's assessment. The Ombudsman made several recommendations about how the Council could improve its short break procedures.

Overnight care

http://www.lgo.org.uk/decisions/children-s-care-services/disabled-children/13-003-902

A woman complained that the council failed to provide an adequate replacement care package for her disabled daughter, after an overnight care package for one weekend a month broke down in June 2009. The Ombudsman found that the lack of provision caused the family a serious injustice because they missed out on the opportunity to spend dedicated time together over a three year period. It recommended the council pay the mother £7,500 (£2,500 a year) to remedy the injustice.

Children in care

Placement too far from family

http://www.lgo.org.uk/decisions/children-s-care-services/looked-after-children/15-003-629

A woman complained that between 2011 and 2016 the council failed to find a placement for her disabled son within a distance that allowed the family to visit regularly, despite her having given it details of more suitable local placements. She also said the council failed to make appropriate plans for her son's current and long-term needs. The council agreed to pay £500 to be held for the child for its failures to consider the child's wishes and failings. It agreed to pay the woman £1500 for the significant avoidable stress and delay and £250 for the time and trouble of the complaint. The council also agreed to arrange training for staff and consider its policies.

Failure to help with immigration status

http://www.lgo.org.uk/decisions/children-s-care-services/looked-after-children/13-019-106

The LGSCO found that Royal Borough of Greenwich failed to act appropriately and in a timely manner to help a young woman regularise her immigration status after she became a looked after child. The council agreed to action the following:

- Apologise for its identified failings.
- Pay the complainant £5,000 to acknowledge the distress caused by the failure to provide consistent support and advice to her as a looked after child, and by the uncertainty caused that, if it were not for those faults, her application to the Home Office for leave to remain in the UK would have been as a child, which may have given her a greater chance of success. This amount also included a sum to acknowledge the time and trouble caused because the council failed to consider her complaint as fully as it should have.
- Provide specialist advice and guidance to its social work staff on the different requirements of the immigration rules.
- Devise an action plan to ensure it gave full and proper consideration to its duties to all its 'looked after children' who may be in need of legal advice.
- To ensure officers record both the questions raised and any legal advice given.
- Ensure all of the complaints it has considered at Stage 1 of the statutory Children Act complaints procedure were progressed to Stage 2 if that is the complainant's wish, as is their right.

Failure to arrange suitable placement (joint complaint with a healthcare trust)

http://www.lgo.org.uk/decisions/children-s-care-services/fostering/14-014-664

The Ombudsmen found that a council failed to arrange a suitable therapeutic placement for a looked after child within a timely manner, and did not provide enough education for many months. In addition, a trust did not make timely referrals for specialist services and did not always provide full appointments.

These faults had a significant impact on the child and his foster parents. The Ombudsmen recommended that:

- the council pay £4000 in recognition of the missed schooling (based on a rate of £300 per month)
- the council pay £1000 to the foster carers for the avoidable stress caused by the delay in arranging a placement
- the trust pay the foster carers £500 for the stress caused by its failure to provide appropriate support in a timely manner.

Age assessment

http://www.lgo.org.uk/decisions/children-s-care-services/other/14-012-369

The council delayed in assessing Mr R's age and failed to make adequate enquiries to ascertain the authenticity of his birth certificate. It assessed his age as three years older than he really was. This caused him a significant injustice as he missed out on appropriate education and was placed in inappropriate accommodation. The Ombudsman recommended the council pay Mr R £500 in recognition of the stress and anxiety suffered, £6000 for his loss of four years' education and £3000 for not receiving age appropriate services for three years.

Care leavers

University costs

http://www.lgo.org.uk/decisions/children-s-care-services/looked-after-children/16-009-920

The LGSCO considered a claim brought by Miss X against Lancashire County Council. Miss X was a care leaver who complained that the council failed to pay her financial support to retake her final year at university after she was unable to complete her third year due to mental health and relationship problems.
A charity paid for Miss X's course fees. Miss X moved to cheaper social housing but said she was left with significant debt. The council agreed to pay Miss X the accommodation costs Miss X incurred – £3,879.

Failure to provide sufficient support when leaving care

http://www.lgo.org.uk/decisions/children-s-care-services/looked-after-children/14-018-019#point4

Mr X, a vulnerable young person, brought a claim against the London Borough of Croydon. The LGSCO found that the council failed to provide Mr X with sufficient support when he left care. This had caused Mr X a great deal of uncertainty and distress. The council failed to comply with recommendations made by an independent investigator despite agreeing with his findings in relation to the complaint. The council agreed to pay Mr X £3,000 to help Mr X secure private rented accommodation and £750 for the distress and uncertainty caused by its failure to make payments for his bed and breakfast accommodation, delay in securing permanent accommodation as well as the time and trouble caused in having to complain to the Ombudsman.

Child protection

Supervised contact

http://www.lgo.org.uk/decisions/children-s-care-services/child-protection/14-003-948

Miss C complained about the way the council oversaw contact arrangements with her mother, whilst she was living with her grandparents. She felt that her wishes and feelings had not been listened to. The Ombudsman found that the council maintained strict contact conditions longer than was necessary and recommended that Miss C and her brother receive £500 each to remedy the injustice.

Failure to investigate child abuse allegations

http://www.lgo.org.uk/decisions/children-s-care-services/child-protection/16-001-936#point5

Ms B, an adult who was previously looked after by Bristol City Council, complained in 2014 about the council's investigation into historic abuse she suffered at home, neglect at the foster placement and the council's failure to investigate allegations of sexual abuse. The LGSCO found that there was fault in the way the council investigated allegations of historic abuse. However the LGSCO did not find fault in the council's decision not to interview the guardian in its investigation of the complaint. The council agreed to apologise to Ms B for its failure to properly investigate the referrals relating to Ms C, its delay in taking action and its failure to properly address the allegations of sexual abuse. The Council paid £1,000 to Ms B for its failures in its investigations of Ms C and £200 to Ms B for its failures in relation to the sexual abuse allegations. The council agreed to pay a further £800 to Ms B to reflect the injustice suffered as a result of the council's failure to properly respond to the sexual abuse allegations.

Adoption – failure in decision-making and failure to explain reasons for its decision

http://www.lgo.org.uk/decisions/children-s-care-services/adoption/14-010-709

The council had decided on the payment of an adoption allowance to Mr B and Ms C but then changed its decision. The council failed to explain the reasons for its decisions and wrongly said that Mr B and Ms C were financially motivated. There was then a delay before this decision was overturned and the children moved in with Mr B and Ms C. The Ombudsman recommended the council pay the complainants £4200 to cover the adoption allowance they would have received had the children moved in when originally anticipated. It also recommended the council pay £1000 in recognition of the stress caused to both the children and Mr B and Ms C. It further advised that the Ombudsman's report should be circulated to anyone who had been told that a decision had been made that Mr B and Ms C were financially motivated.

Failure to manage and support foster carer

http://www.lgo.org.uk/decisions/children-s-care-services/looked-after-children/13-018-819#point5

The LGSCO considered a claim against Dudley Metropolitan Borough Council. The LGSCO found that the council failed to properly manage various aspects of Mrs B's case when she provided foster care to child A. The council agreed to put in place a detailed action plan to deal with the faults identified by the stage two investigator. The council apologised to Mrs B, agreed to pay her legal fees and offered her £1,750 compensation.

Failure to provide carer with adequate information

http://www.lgo.org.uk/decisions/children-s-care-services/looked-after-children/13-010-800#point6

The LGSCO found that in this case Birmingham City Council failed to provide Mrs X with adequate information about the financial implications of caring for her granddaughter, N, when N's mother was unable to do so. The council's decision that N could no longer live with her mother put Mrs X under pressure to care for her and she lost out financially when the council decided it was a private arrangement. The council agreed to backdate the payments it had made for N from the date of the child protection conference, less any payments already made during that period. The council also agreed to pay Mrs X an additional £250 for her time and trouble in having to approach the Ombudsman to secure a remedy. This was because she should not have had to do so when the council's own investigation had already upheld her complaint that it had failed to provide her with adequate funding to look after N.

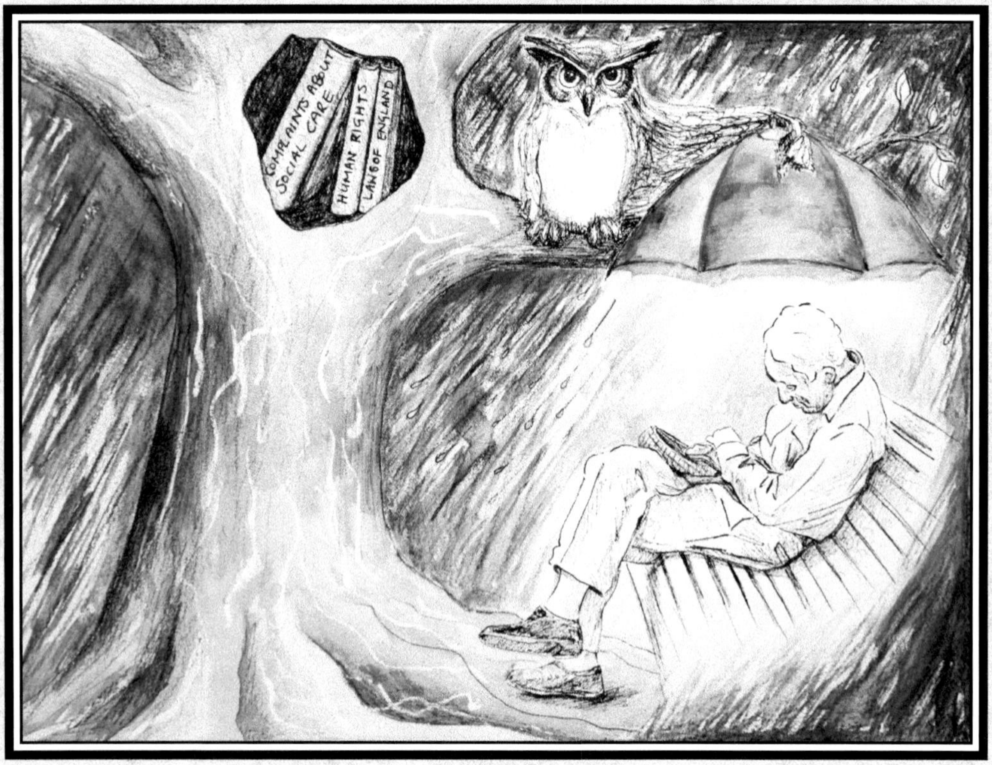
COMPLAINTS ABOUT
SOCIAL CARE
HUMAN RIGHTS
LAW OF ENGLAND

Chapter 5: Complaints about social care

5.1: Overview

This chapter covers adult social services, and this includes; transitions from children's services to adult services; assessments, equipment and adaptations provided for chronically sick and disabled persons; and adult social care providers (private companies providing adult social services such as residential homes).

It is important to realise that very often social care institutions work together. An example would be the local authority and a local NHS institution providing support to people with disabilities. Alternatively, it might be two local authorities working together to support the same person. The complaints system obliges institutions to work together and cooperate to resolve complaints.

5.2: The complaints system for social care

The legislation that sets out the complaints procedures for social care is contained in S114 of the Health and Social Care Act (Community Health and Standards) (2003) and the Local Authority Social Services and National Health Service Complaints Regulations (2009).

S114 of the Health and Social Care Act (2003) sets up a complaints system for social services. Once again this is quite separate from the Children Act (1989) complaints system for children in care and children in need, which is discussed in Chapter 4. A 'child in need' will include a child with disability or any child whose health or development is compromised without social care. Consequently, it is difficult to envisage a situation where a child is covered by the 2009 regulations. Nonetheless those regulations refer specifically to situations that involve children. When advocating for a child, it is best to make the complaint under the Children Act (1989) procedure, where the procedure is more robust.

S114(1)(b) of the act says that the system will also apply to independent contractors, such as charities who carry out work on behalf of local authorities.

This means that the complaint still goes to the local authority even though the work was carried out by a charity or an independent company.

Finally, local authorities are required under the Chronically Sick and Disabled Persons Act (1970) to provide support to the long-term sick and the disabled. Typically, they do this by providing specialist assessments for community equipment and adaptations. Although the assessments are carried out by the local NHS Service, S114(1)(c) of the 2003 act extends the complaints system to this kind of work. This is one area where the advocate will need to consider whether to bring the complaint against the local NHS Service or against the local authority, or both. For instance, if the assessment carried by the NHS Service is faulty, then the complaint should be submitted to the NHS. If, however, there is a problem with the provision of the equipment, then the complaint should be submitted to the local authority. If in any doubt, advocates can submit the complaint to both institutions, who are required to work together to resolve the complaint.

As we have noted in Chapter 3, it is a very useful to mention the legal basis for any complaint at the start of the process. So for instance, a complaint about a faulty assessment of a disabled person's need for equipment would be brought under S114(1)(c) of the 2003 act. Advocates can rely on this kind of reference to underscore the legitimacy of the complaint.

5.3: Independent advocacy under the Care Act (2014)

Section 67 of the Care Act (2014) states that a local authority must, in certain circumstances, arrange for a person who is independent of the authority (an 'independent advocate') to be available to represent and support an individual adult's involvement in:

- care assessments
- care and support planning
- care and support reviews
- safeguarding.

The circumstances that apply are where the local authority considers that the individual would experience substantial difficulty in:

- understanding relevant information

- retaining that information
- using or weighing that information
- communicating their views, wishes or feelings (whether by talking, using sign language or any other means).

The 2014 act is accompanied by regulations contained in the Care and Support (Independent Advocacy Support) (No 2) Regulations (2014). Regulation 2 sets out the requirements a person must meet in order to be an independent advocate. Regulation 5 sets out the manner in which independent advocates must perform their functions. Regulation 6 is about how a local authority is to work with an independent advocate.

The government has also issued guidance on the Care Act (2014): https://www.gov.uk/government/publications/care-act-statutory-guidance/care-and-support-statutory-guidance#safeguarding-1.

Chapter 7 of care and support statutory guidance issued by the Department of Health deals with the issue of independent advocacy and how it is intended to work: https://www.gov.uk/government/uploads/system/uploads/attachment_data/file/315993/Care-Act-Guidance.pdf.

The guidance makes the point that many of the people who qualify for advocacy under the Care Act (2014) will also qualify for advocacy under the Mental Capacity Act (2005) (See Chapter 6). The same advocate can provide support as an advocate under the Care Act as under the Mental Capacity Act.

This kind of advocacy is commonly provided by charities and commissioned by local authorities.

5.4: The Local Authority Social Services and National Health Service Complaints (England) Regulations (2009)

These are the regulations that specify how the complaints system is to work. We will see in Chapter 6 that these regulations also apply to complaints about the NHS, and one of them (Regulation 7) only applies to the NHS. We will now examine the important parts of the regulations, which apply to local authorities.

5.4.1: General principles for dealing with complaints

Regulation 3(2) states that the arrangements for dealing with complaints must be such as to ensure that:

- complaints are dealt with efficiently
- complaints are properly investigated
- complainants are treated with respect and courtesy
- complainants receive, so far as is reasonably practical, assistance to enable them to understand the procedure in relation to complaints or advice on where they may obtain such assistance
- complainants receive a timely and appropriate response
- complainants are told the outcome of the investigation of their complaint
- action is taken, if necessary, in the light of the outcome of a complaint.

These are the fundamental building blocks behind the local authority complaints process and it is useful to be able to remind local authorities of their existence.

5.4.2: The complaints manager

Regulation 4 says that the local authority must designate two types of person; firstly a 'responsible person' who ensures compliance with the regulations; and secondly 'a complaints manager' to actually manage the procedure. In a local authority, the responsible person is the chief executive.

Complaints are often submitted to front-line workers or team managers because it is not always clear that there is a complaints manager and what their contact details are. Advocates should make sure that their client's complaint is seen by the complaints manager.

5.4.3: Who can make a complaint?

Regulation 5 tells us who may make a complaint. This can be either a person who receives or has received services from the local authority. It can also be a person who is affected, or likely to be affected, by the action, omission or decision of the local authority. Regulation 5(2) allows a complaint to be made by a representative (or advocate), which might be someone who is acting on behalf of a person who has died, who is a child, is physically or mentally incapable, or who has requested the representative to act on their behalf.

Under Regulation 5(3), the local authority can refuse to consider the complaint of a child brought through a representative, if it is not satisfied that there are reasonable grounds for the complaint being made by a representative instead of the child. If this happens, the local authority must notify the representative in writing and state the reason for its decision.

Regulations 5(4) and 5(5) state that the local authority can also refuse to consider complaints which are brought by representatives on behalf of children or those who lack mental capacity, if it feels the representative is not acting in the complainants' best interests.

5.4.4: Complaints which are excluded

Regulation 8 provides a list of those complaints, which are excluded from consideration. It is useful to know that these include:

- a complaint that is made orally and which is resolved to the complainant's satisfaction within one working day
- a complaint which has previously been investigated under the regulations or a previous complaints procedure
- a complaint arising out of the alleged failure by a responsible body to comply with a request for information under the Freedom of Information Act (2000) (See Chapter 12).

A complaint that is the subject of a civil compensation claim or criminal process is not excluded by the regulations as it is under the Children Act (1989) Representations Procedure (England) Regulations (2006), which we considered in Chapter 4. However, if the matter goes to the Local Government and Social Care Ombudsman, this kind of matter (i.e. a civil compensation claim or something subject to criminal proceedings) will be outside the remit of the Ombudsman's Scheme.

As we saw in Chapter 3, mistakes made by local authorities in relation to children and adults can sometimes form the subject of compensation claims, which are brought through the civil courts. These can prove very expensive, not least because the award of compensation is accompanied by legal costs (which can be as much as, if not more than, the actual compensation amount). On the other hand, a complaint may cost the local authority very much less. There are situations where the complaints process is in fact the best way forward because it is quicker and less costly for the complainant. At the end of this chapter, we set out some examples of those cases that have been put before the Local Government and Social Care Ombudsman and it can be seen that some of the recommended compensation awards are quite high.

This is one of those matters on which advice should be taken by a solicitor specialising in compensation claims brought against social services by adults.

It is important to bear in mind what we saw in Chapter 3 about the limits to the remit of the Local Government and Social Care Ombudsman. According to S26(6) and Schedule 5 of the Local Government Act (1974), the LGSCO cannot investigate issues where there are other legal processes available.

5.4.5: Local authorities must co-operate with each other when handling complaints

Regulation 9 enables two local authorities, or two 'responsible bodies' to handle a complaint which involves both of them. It says that they have to co-operate, agree who is to take the lead in co-ordinating the handling of the complaint and communicating with the complainant. They must also give the complainant a co-ordinated response.

This is a useful provision to use to avoid being bounced between two or more authorities who are attempting to pass the buck elsewhere. In these situations, advocates would be advised to ensure that both parties are copied into all correspondence. This is also an example of a situation where it may be possible to seek the advice and intervention of the Local Government and Social Care Ombudsman prior to the complaints procedure being exhausted.

5.4.6: Adult social care providers

Regulation 11 applies where the complaint is made to an 'adult social care provider'. This is someone who is providing care under Part 1 of the Health and Social Care Act (2008), for example, residential homes and respite centres. Local authorities use independent contractors to deliver care and these providers have to be approved under the 2008 act.

Where a complaint is about an adult social care provider, then the local authority must ask the complainant whether they consent to the complaint being sent to that provider and, if they do, must send those details to the provider as soon as possible. However the complaint is still the local authority's responsibility and has to be handled by the local authority. Regulation 11(3) states that the local authority then has to explain to the complainant what part of the complaint it will handle and then co-operate with the provider.

5.4.7: Time limit for complainants

Regulation 12 sets out the time limit for making a complaint. Briefly the time limit is 12 months. The regulation says that the complaint must be made no later than 12 months after the date on which the matter which is the subject of the complaint occurred or, if later, the date on which the matter which is the subject of the complaint came to the notice of the complainant. The writers believe that this means that the clock starts running when the complainant realises that 'something has gone wrong' rather than realising that they had the right to complain. However, they also advise that ideally complaints should be brought as soon as possible.

The local authority can waive the time limit if it is satisfied that the complainant had good reasons for not making the complaint within that time limit. It must also still be possible to investigate the complaint effectively and fairly. So if, for example, the complaint centres around an unrecorded incident with a certain member of staff, who has now left the department, it may not be possible to investigate the complaint at all even if the institution tried.

5.4.8: The initial procedure for dealing with the complaint

Regulation 13 sets out the initial procedure to be followed when the complaint first goes in. First of all, a complaint may be made orally, in writing or electronically, i.e. by email. The local authority has to acknowledge the complaint (orally or in writing) within 3 working days, except where the complaint should be directed elsewhere. Acknowledgement is important because it is not unknown for local authorities to deny ever receiving the complaint and advocates may need to chase this response if it is not forthcoming.

When the local authority acknowledges the complaint, it must offer to discuss with the complainant, at a time to be agreed:

- the manner in which the complaint is to be handled
- the period within which the investigation of the complaint is likely to be completed
- when its response to the complaint is likely to be sent out.

The complainant does not have to agree to this offer of a discussion. If there is no agreement, the responsible body must determine, on its own, the response period for dealing with the complaint and notify the complainant in writing of that period.

Once again, it is important to make a note of the response period set out by the local authority because complaints processes (particularly in local authorities) are often delayed past the time limits set up by the regulations. It is possible to obtain a separate award of compensation solely for this delay.

Regulation 14 then sets out the next stage of the complaints procedure. A local authority must investigate the complaint speedily and efficiently. During the investigation it must keep the complainant updated as far as reasonably practicable.

On completion, the local authority must send the complainant a response in writing, signed by the responsible person (the chief executive or someone authorised by them), which includes:

- A report explaining how the complaint has been considered and the conclusions. It should address any matters, which the complaint specifies, or which the local authority has considered.

- Confirmation of whether the local authority agrees to take any action in consequence of the complaint or whether any action has already been taken.

- Details of the complainant's right to take their complaint to the Local Government and Social Care Ombudsman

5.4.9: The time limit for processing the complaint

Regulation 14(4) says that if the local authority does not send the complainant a response within 6 months of receiving the complaint, then it must notify the complainant in writing and explain the reason why. Thereafter it must send the response as soon as is reasonably practicable. As noted above, delay is a feature of local authority complaints processes, which is why it is important to hold these local authorities to the timescale and remind them of Regulation 14.

5.5: Varying policies between local authorities

The regulations do not specify that the complaints procedure has to be anything more than the kind of response outlined above. However local authorities have designed their own complaints procedures, which have different stages. Obviously, a complainant or their advocate needs to have some familiarity with those procedures. Published procedures vary widely between local authorities and the advocate should check with the relevant local authority. We now look at two such procedures.

The London Borough of Camden's complaints procedure is published on the 'council and democracy' section of their website. Their procedure for complaints about adult social care makes specific reference to the 2009 regulations. This procedure is described as having only one stage but Camden have developed a system of dealing with complaints depending on their complexity and seriousness. Very briefly, complaints are acknowledged and then classified into low, medium, high and extreme impact, according to their significance for service users and the service. A triage system is used to 'score' the complaint. Depending on that score, the complaint is then dealt with progressively in ways that are increasingly formal and independent. A 'complaint plan' is drawn up which identifies the level of complexity of the complaint and how the complaint will be handled. Medium and high complaints will usually be dealt with through an independent investigation. More complex complaints and those categorised as high and extreme will be addressed through investigation by someone completely independent of the service concerned. There is an appeal process for complainants who are dissatisfied with the response that they get from Camden. Finally, Camden notifies the complainant of their right to go to the Local Government and Social Care Ombudsman.

By contrast the published adult social care complaints procedure for Cumbria County Council is presented in a very much simpler way but it appears to use similar methods. Cumbria makes use of a 'complaints resolution plan' to set out a pathway for the progress of the complaint. That plan might mean a review of a support plan, an investigation by a lead manager or an independently chaired meeting. In exceptional circumstances, where the facts are in dispute, an external independent investigation can be commissioned. As with Camden, Cumbria notifies the complainant of their right to approach the Local Government and Social Care Ombudsman.

Regulation 16 says that the 'responsible body', i.e. the local authority, must make information available to the public about its arrangements for dealing with complaints.

5.6: Key points

- The legislation that sets out the complaints procedures for social care is contained in S114 of the Health and Social Care Act (2003) and the Local Authority Social Services and National Health Service Complaints Regulations (2009).

- People who can use this procedure to complain are; those receiving or who have received social care; those who may be affected by the acts or omissions of the social care provider (for example, a carer); disabled children; and representatives of the aforementioned persons.

- Typical complaints falling under these procedures may concern (but are certainly not limited to): domiciliary care, residential care, assessments, care plans, direct payments, safeguarding, transition planning, transport, and disabled-facilities grants.

- The complaint must generally be submitted within one year, although exceptions may apply.

- If the complaint is made orally and then resolved within one working day, the institution need not consider it further.

- The institution must acknowledge the complaint within 3 working days. The institution should try to talk with the complainant and agree the time-period for response. In any case, they must put the determined time period in writing to the complainant.

- The institution should try to investigate the complaint as swiftly as possible and keep the complainant updated. If it has not completed its investigation within 6 months, it must write to the complainant explaining the delay.

- The complaint response should be in writing. It should include a report about the investigation, any proposed actions the institution will take, and details about how to escalate the complaint to the Local Government and Social Care Ombudsman.

- When a complaint involves more than one institution, the institutions must work together to resolve the complaint.

- Remember that the Local Government and Social Care Ombudsman may be approached if the local authority does not follow the complaints procedure or does not respond in time.

- Different institutions may have developed their own policies, which must follow the act and regulations. These institutions are then responsible for making any such policies available to potential complainants.

5.7: Case studies from the Local Government and Social Care Ombudsman

As we saw in Chapter 4, the Local Government and Social Care Ombudsman's (LGSCO) website has a facility for searching decisions: http://www.lgo.org.uk/decisions.

We now consider a number of complaint reports. Once again, it important to realise that the remedies recommended by the Ombudsman are not restricted to compensation but also include remedies such as an apology or reinstatement of services. For each report, we have put the website page.

A website has been set up in conjunction with the writing of this book, to assist advocates in working out the kind of remedies that are appropriate for a particular complaint. This can be found at: http://www.complaintadvocates.co.uk/.

Failure to provide support and resources at home

http://www.lgo.org.uk/decisions/adult-care-services/domiciliary-care/13-000-109#Main

This was a complaint against Tameside Metropolitan Borough Council brought by Mrs X. The complaint related to the council's failure to deal properly with the support it provided to Mrs X's mother, Mrs Y. The council agreed to apologise to Mrs X and Mrs Y; allocate a senior manager to rebuild the relationship with Mrs X and Mrs Y; and allocate a new social worker, not previously involved, to work with Mrs Y. This included a minimum of four visits over two months until the relationship was rebuilt and Mrs Y was confident in knowing what resources were available to her. The Ombudsman also recommended the council pay Mrs Y £2,000 for the injustice caused to her; to refund amounts of £316 and £391, which were charges raised against her in error; and to pay Mrs X £2,000 for the injustice it caused her.

Failure to follow home care policy and neglect

http://www.lgo.org.uk/decisions/adult-care-services/domiciliary-care/14-007-485#Main

The LGSCO considered a complaint against Rochdale Metropolitan Borough Council, brought by Mrs X on behalf of her mother Mrs Y, who at the time of the complaint was deceased. Mrs Y had advanced dementia and needed full support with all aspects of care. The allegation was that the carers engaged by the council dropped Mrs Y while moving her at home, causing her a broken femur. This breached the care agency's policies and was neglectful. After the fall, the carers failed to seek medical assistance and left an inaccurate care visit record. The above-mentioned failures caused significant injustice to Mrs X. Furthermore, the uncertainty (whether the moving of her mother worsened the injury) caused Mrs X unnecessary additional distress at a time when she had to cope with her mother's death. The council had also failed to provide appropriate support for the family after Mrs Y's discharge from hospital. The council took far too long to complete the safeguarding investigation. The LGSCO recommended that the actions detailed in the decision should ensure a better experience for other families in the future. The council agreed to apologise to Mrs X for the failures that had been identified and to pay her £1,500, consisting of:

- £1,000 for the distress to her feelings caused by the way Mrs Y was treated after the fall
- £250 for the uncertainty she has been left with about how the fall happened
- £250 for the prolongation of her distress by the delayed safeguarding investigation.

Residential care – poor assessment and overcharging

http://www.lgo.org.uk/decisions/adult-care-services/residential-care/15-005-577#Main

This was a claim brought by Ms B against Kingsmead Care Home Limited. The allegation was regarding the care provider's failure to carry out a proper pre-admission assessment of Ms B's mother. In the case, the LGSCO found that the care provider carried out two readmission assessments and agreed it could care for Ms B's mother, Mrs C. When Mrs C moved to the care home, she was diagnosed with dementia and her behaviour was not manageable. Therefore Ms B was asked to find an alternative home for Mrs C but until then the care provider agreed to put in extra care to keep Mrs C safe. The care provider charged for this extra care, without informing Ms B about its extra care charges. Ms B was surprised to receive the invoice for more than the agreed fees. To quickly resolve the complaint, both parties have agreed a refund of some of the fees. The amount of £3,118 was refunded to Mrs C.

Residential care – safeguarding issues that resulted in changes to policy

http://www.lgo.org.uk/decisions/adult-care-services/residential-care/13-008-287#Main

The LGSCO found that Caring Homes Healthcare Group Limited was at fault because it did not do enough to keep Mrs Y safe. The LGSCO recommended that the care provider apologise to Mrs Y's daughter, Mrs X, detailing the faults identified in the LGSCO's statement and that a copy of the apology be provided to the Ombudsman within one month. The Ombudsman also recommended that the company refund £2,600 to Mrs Y's estate to remedy the injustice to her. Further, it recommended that the company ensure that; safeguarding policy and procedures, risk assessment policy and procedures, falls prevention and post-falls protocol were up to date; all staff receive training, or refresher training within 3 months; all staff receive ongoing support through regular updates and supervision; and copies of these to be provided to the Ombudsman within 3 months as evidence of training provided.

Assessment and care plan – 2 year delay in providing for personal needs

http://www.lgo.org.uk/decisions/adult-care-services/assessment-and-care-plan/11-009-273

This was a claim brought against Birmingham City Council after it took more than two years to provide for Mr N's needs. Mr N had a severe learning disability, epilepsy and atypical autism. Mr N's epilepsy meant that he had seizures of varying severity and needed help with daily living. The LGSCO found maladministration causing injustice and therefore the Council agreed to pay Mr N £52,513 for lost payments and services and to further pay £500 to Mr N's mother and sister in recognition of the time and inconvenience they had in trying to get adequate services for Mr N.

Assessment and care plan – paper-based and inaccurate assessment

http://www.lgo.org.uk/decisions/adult-care-services/assessment-and-care-plan/14-005-981#Main

The LGSCO considered a claim against North Somerset Council and the Trust. Mr and Mrs L complained about a desktop assessment that was carried out by two social workers. In the assessment Mr and Mrs L were accused of physical, emotional and financial abuse of their daughter Miss L. The complainants alleged that mental health services were withdrawn from Miss L because of this assessment and that, as a result, Miss L's care was adversely affected. Overall the desktop assessment had caused considerable distress to the whole family. The LGSCO found that the assessment was flawed. The information contained in it was so inaccurate that it could not be relied upon. Further the inaccurate information led to staff wrongly diagnosing that Miss L did not have a mental health need. Mr and Mrs L have offered Miss L a significant amount of emotional and financial support. Due to the flawed assessment, Miss L was exposed to a great risk and Mr and Mrs L suffered significant distress. The LGSCO recommended the below:

- The trust to remove the assessment from all its records and that, within a month, the Council would ensure it does the same.

- Within a month, the trust and council would apologise unreservedly to Miss L and Mr and Mrs L for the lasting impact the flawed assessment had created.

- Within the next three months, the trust and the council should produce an action plan to address the faults identified in the report. Copies of this action plan should be sent to Mr and Mrs L, the Ombudsmen and various other involved institutions.

- Within the next three months, the trust and the council should jointly make payments of £10,000 to Mr and Mrs L in recognition of the injustices they have suffered. This amount should be split evenly with £5,000 being provided by the trust and £5,000 being provided by the council.

Delay in payment, provision of equipment and care planning

http://www.lgo.org.uk/decisions/adult-care-services/direct-payments/13-015-351#Main

The council delayed putting in place adequate services to meet Mr B's adult social care needs. Mr B requested the direct payments in June 2011 but the council only put the direct payments in place 2 years after Mr B's request. The council's failure had had a significant impact on Mr B. The council agreed to apologise to Mr B and pay to Mr B the amount of £18,000 to recognise the impact on Mr B of not having direct payments in place for the full period of November 2011 until June 2013. In addition the council paid a further £3,000 in recognition of the impact of its failures in care planning, arranging the lifting and handling of equipment, delay in changing the social worker and delay in complaint handling. The council had also agreed to take any learning points from this complaint and feedback to relevant staff, to prevent a recurrence of the identified delays. Lastly, it agreed to put in place adequate supervision of Mr Bs case to restore Mr B's confidence.

Joint complaint against the local authority and the healthcare trust

http://www.lgo.org.uk/decisions/adult-care-services/direct-payments/14-006-021

This was a complaint brought from a woman about the way the trust and the council dealt with her application for a personal budget (self-directed support). The allegation was that the trust and the council failed to promptly provide a remedy to the woman after her complaint was upheld in March 2014. As a result the woman, a double amputee with significant mental health issues, had not had access to appropriate social care support for more than 12 months. She also had the added stress of continuing to pursue a complaint which should have been resolved sooner. The council and the trust agreed to:

- Write to the woman, within one month, to apologise for the faults identified, and the distress these faults caused.
- Reimburse £14,000 to the woman for the costs she incurred in buying support that should properly have come from her self-directed support (SDS) budget, covering the period January 2014 to February 2015 inclusive.
- Agree her monthly SDS as a matter of urgency and ensure that payments were made within three months at the latest, and backdated appropriately.
- Pay her £12,000 to acknowledge the impact on her of not having an adequate SDS budget in place (by considering the woman's vulnerability, the impact on her daily life, and the length of time she had been affected).
- Pay the women a further £1,000 to acknowledge the avoidable stress and frustration, and her justifiable outrage, from having to pursue her complaint.
- Disregard these payments when assessing her financial contributions to her SDS budget.
- Produce an action plan within three months addressing the faults listed within the report and setting out what action has and will be taken to address them.

The LGSCO considered a claim against Birmingham City Council. Due to the Council's failure to make the proper transitional arrangements for Ms A's care, in time for her to start university as planned, Ms A had to defer the start of her course for a year. The council found that there were long delays and no action was taken to progress Ms A's transitional arrangements. As a result, Ms A suffered significant disappointment as well as the upset of making different arrangements for her care for the intervening year. The council agreed to apologise to Ms A and to make her a payment of £5,000 to acknowledge the significant effect of its delays.

Failure to arrange respite after transition from children's services to adult services

http://www.lgo.org.uk/decisions/adult-care-services/transition-from-childrens-services/15-020-374#point5

This was a claim brought against Lincolnshire County Council by Mrs X, which involved the council's failure to ensure a smooth transition from children's services to adult care services for the complainant's daughter. Mrs X's daughter had severe autism, learning difficulties, a number of health conditions and some behavioural problems. The LGSCO found that, even though the daughter had a high level of complex needs, the council had delayed in arranging overnight respite care for her following the transition from children's to adult services and failed to make any provision for the year. As a result the daughter's family had not had a break from caring and Mrs X became exhausted and struggled to cope. Further the council failed to properly communicate with Mrs X. The council agreed to make the payment of £4,881.60 to Mrs X, which represented half of the cost of overnight carers at home; to apologise to Mrs X for its failures to provide overnight respite care; and to review its processes.

Care needs and lost earnings

www.lgo.org.uk/assets/attach/2037/12-007-311-Shropshire-11.04.2013.pdf

The LGSCO considered a complaint against Shropshire County Council, brought by a married couple. The wife had complex mental health needs requiring 24-hour care and lived at home where she was supported by her husband. Shropshire failed to carry out a proper assessment of her needs and provided direct payments for only 50 hours per week of care for her husband, who was forced to leave his job. In this case, the LGSCO was not prepared to compensate the husband for his lost earnings, pension and career prospects. The LGSCO said that it would be too difficult to get an accurate picture of how much work he could have done; how much he had lost by way of pension or whether he would have remained in that employment. The Ombudsman recommended that the council:

- made a payment of £61,270 to the husband in recognition of the care he provided which was not funded by the council at the appropriate time
- provided an apology to the couple about the time that it had taken to deal with the complaint
- reviewed its procedures for complaint handling in light of comments made in this report
- paid the wife £1000 for the time and trouble in making the complaint and the further delay in obtaining the remedy.

Transport – delay in providing blue badge

http://www.lgo.org.uk/decisions/adult-care-services/transport/15-008-607#point5

This was a complaint brought against Cornwall Council. Mr A complained that the council delayed to process his application for a blue badge. As a result this caused Mr A inconvenience and avoidable parking expenses. The LGSCO found that the council was at fault for not issuing Mr A with a blue badge because it had evidence and the application fee. The council agreed to pay Mr A £300.

Transport – misleading information given by council

http://www.lgo.org.uk/decisions/adult-care-services/transport/13-019-834#Main

Mr B complained against London Borough of Harrow on behalf of his son, Mr C, who had several medical conditions, including epilepsy, dyspraxia, Crohn's disease, short bowel syndrome, joint pain and osteoporosis. Mr C also had learning difficulties. Mr B complained that the council unreasonably refused Mr C's application for a taxi card and failed to consider Mr C's medical conditions. The LGSCO found that the council was not at fault for refusing Mr C's application for a taxi card. However the council provided misleading information about the criteria for the scheme to Mr C. The council agreed to reword the eligibility criteria for taxi cards on its website, agreed to apologise to Mr C and to pay Mr C £100 compensation to reflect the time and trouble Mr C had to go in pursuing his compliant.

Disabled Facilities Grants – failure to comply with Ombudsman's recommendations

http://www.lgo.org.uk/decisions/adult-care-services/disabled-facilities-grants/14-017-085#point5

This was a complaint brought against Birmingham City Council by Mr X. The LGSCO found that the council failed to comply with the Ombudsman's recommendations in Mr X's previous complaint. Further, the council significantly delayed in providing adaptations to meet Mr X's son's needs. Lastly, the LGSCO found that the council delayed in instructing a surveyor to inspect Mr X's property. The council agreed to take actions to ensure the work to Mr X's home would be completed in a timely manner and to pay Mr X £750 for his time and trouble pursuing his complaint as well as the distress and uncertainty caused by the council's continued failings in delivering adaptations for his disabled son.

Disabled Facilities Grants – failure to provide information

http://www.lgo.org.uk/decisions/adult-care-services/disabled-facilities-grants/14-018-384#point5

Ms Z complained against Barrow-in-Furness Borough Council. The LGSCO found that even though the council considered Ms Z's referral for a Disabled Facilities Grant (DFG) appropriately, relying on the occupation therapist's assessment, the council failed to provide information about DFGs or other funding alternatives, or to keep in touch with Ms Z during periods of delay. As a result Ms Z suffered distress and frustration. The council's failure put Ms Z to unnecessary time and trouble. The council agreed to apologise to Ms Z for failing to tell her about the DFG process or other funding options, and for failing to update her during the reassessment and complaint processes. It agreed to pay Ms Z £500 for her avoidable distress and frustration and her undue time and trouble in continuing the matter. It would also consult with the agencies involved in the DFG process to provide clear information about alternative funding to a DFG and then provide a copy of its literature pack and alternative funding leaflet to the Ombudsman within three months.

Failure to deal with complaint about drop-in service

http://www.LGSCO.org.uk/decisions/adult-care-services/other/15-019-386#point6

Mr H complained that London Borough of Enfield failed to deal with his complaint made about its drop-in service. The council accepted that it did not deal properly with Mr H's complaint. The council did not respond properly to Mr H until after the LGSCO wrote to it. The council offered to pay Mr H £450 as a remedy for the injustice caused to him.

ATHENE
MEDICAL
CLINIC
REASONABLE STANDARD
OF CARE
SAFEGUARDING
TRUST
HELP
KINDNESS
HIPPOCRATIC
OATH
ALL SPECIES
WELCOME
NO DISCRIMINATION
DUTY OF CARE
GOOD MEDICAL PRACTICE

Chapter 6: Complaints about health services

6.1: The Care Quality Commission

The Care Quality Commission (CQC) is the independent regulator for health and social care in England (both public and private) and it was established by the Health and Social Care Act (2008). It makes sure that services such as hospitals, care homes, dentists and GP surgeries provide people with safe, effective, compassionate and high-quality care, and encourages these services to improve. They publish reports on individual providers, which can be seen on their website: www.cqc.org.uk.

The Health and Social Care Act (2008) (Regulated Activities) Regulations (2014) prescribe the kinds of activities that are regulated activities for the purposes of the 2008 act and how those activities should be carried on. Providers of these regulated activities are required to register with the CQC. These requirements apply to all providers of a regulated activity including NHS bodies, independent providers and voluntary sector organisations.

Regulation 20 of the 2014 regulations also introduced one new requirement, which only applies to health service bodies. This is the 'duty of candour', which is a legal duty placed on the NHS to inform and apologise to patients if there have been mistakes in their care that have led to significant harm. The duty aims to help patients receive accurate, truthful information from health providers.

NHS Resolution (which handles claims brought against the NHS) publishes a quick and easy-to-read guide on the duty of candour, which can be found at: http://www.nhsla.com/OtherServices/Documents/NHS%20LA%20-%20Duty%20of%20Candour.pdf.

Part 4 of the 2014 regulations (8 to 20) sets out the fundamental standards of safety and quality. These are standards below which the quality of care must not fall or providers will be in breach of their registration with the CQC. The fundamental standards include requirements to ensure that service users are treated with dignity and respect; receive suitable nutrition; are safeguarded from abuse; and receive care in an environment which is clean and safe. The CQC can take enforcement action against providers that do not meet these standards.

6.2: The constitution and values of the NHS

The majority of health services in England are delivered via the National Health Service (NHS). The Department of Health (DoH) has published a constitution for the NHS. This is a not a very long document and when making a complaint to the NHS, it is worth reading: www.gov.uk/government/publications/the-nhs-constitution-for-england/the-nhs-constitution-for-england.

The constitution sets out seven key principles that guide the NHS in all it does.

1. The NHS provides a comprehensive service, available to all.
2. Access to NHS services is based on clinical need, not an individual's ability to pay.
3. NHS services are free of charge, except in limited circumstances sanctioned by parliament.
4. The NHS aspires to the highest standards of excellence and professionalism.
5. The patient will be at the heart of everything the NHS does.
6. The NHS works across organisational boundaries.
7. The NHS is committed to providing best value for taxpayers' money.

The NHS then has the following values:

- Working together for patients.
- Respect and dignity.
- Commitment to quality of care.
- Compassion.
- Improving lives.
- Everyone counts.

There is also a list of rights and responsibilities for both patients and staff in the NHS. Also on the same part of the DoH website can be found *NHS Complaints Guidance*: www.gov.uk/government/publications/the-nhs-constitution-for-england/how-do-i-give-feedback-or-make-a-complaint-about-an-nhs-service.

6.3: The structure of the NHS

Before we look at how the various complaints systems work, we need to look at the structure of the NHS. This has undergone a great deal of change in recent years, and it is important to understand the various bodies which deliver health services, and the way in which they work together. For instance, local authorities and NHS bodies work together to deliver health services and care. The complaints system is set up to deal with those joint arrangements, so that a complaint can go to the right person.

6.3.1: Trusts, NHS England, clinical commissioning groups and Healthwatch

The Health and Social Care Act (2012) is the statute that gives us our present NHS structure. Under this act, the vast majority of hospitals are run either by trusts or foundation trust, with the intention that all trusts should eventually become foundation trusts. General practitioners, dentists, opticians and other providers of local healthcare are normally self-employed and contract their services back to the NHS.

The act created the NHS Commissioning Board, otherwise known as NHS England. This oversees the budget, planning, delivery, and day-to-day operation of the commissioning side of the NHS in England.

The act also set up clinical commissioning groups, which are responsible for commissioning the majority of health services. They are accountable to NHS England.

A new national body, Healthwatch England, was established as part of the CQC with each local authority being required to establish its own local Healthwatch organisations. This network shares information, expertise and learning in order to improve health and social care services.

The 2012 act is intended to ensure that local authorities and the NHS work together. Each local authority is required to establish 'health and well-being boards', which prepare the joint strategic needs assessment, the joint health and well-being strategy and the promotion of integrated working between NHS, public health and social care commissioners.

Foundation trusts and clinical commissioning groups can also be designated as care trusts. Care trusts are NHS organisations that integrate health and social care and to which local authorities can delegate health-related functions in order to provide integrated local health and social care. All of these bodies appear in the complaints system.

It is confusing that there are so many different bodies but it is important (when making a complaint) to identify the correct organisation against whom the complaint should be directed. For most advocates supporting vulnerable clients, the complaint would be made directly to the healthcare provider, i.e. the NHS trust that owned the hospital.

6.3.2: Protecting public health

The Health and Social Care Act (2012) places a duty on the government to protect public health. This is a different concept from providing health services. Protecting public health includes carrying out research into disease, providing laboratory services, providing information and advice to the public about dangers to health, and providing national vaccination and screening programmes. There is also a duty on the government and local authorities to improve public health. Improving health could include smoking cessation or weight loss services, for example, or the provision of advice and information to help people who want to adopt healthier behaviour. As we will see below, there are now regulations for making a complaint about public health functions under the NHS act.

6.4: The statutory framework for the NHS complaints system

In Chapter 3, we saw how S114 of the Health and Social Care (Community Health and Standards) Act (2003) set out the foundation of the complaints system for social care. The same act applies to NHS complaints.

S113 allows the government to make regulations for the 'handling and consideration of complaints' made to NHS bodies, an NHS body working with a local authority or a NHS commissioning board or a clinical commissioning group.

S115 deals with what will be included in the regulations. S118 allows the complainant to make a complaint to the Health Service Commissioner otherwise known as the Parliamentary and Health Service Ombudsman. S119 allows the complaints investigating body to process a complainant's data without breaching the Data Protection Act (1998).

6.5: Independent advocacy and advice in the NHS

S223A of the Local Government and Public Involvement in Health Act (2007) states that each local authority must make such arrangements as they consider appropriate for the provision of independent advocacy for complaints about health services.

Advocacy services are defined as services providing assistance (whether by way of representation or otherwise) to persons making various types of complaints in relation to the provision of health services, or to persons intending to make such complaints.

These services are commonly provided by charities, and commissioned by local authorities. Enquiries should be directed towards that local authority.

The Parliamentary and Health Service Ombudsman publishes a helpful guide to finding a local advocacy service: https://www.ombudsman.org.uk/making-complaint/getting-advice-and-support.

All NHS hospitals should have an established Patient Advice & Liaison Service (PALS) which acts as an information service for patients and their families/friends. PALS also follows up concerns which may be raised about hospital services on an informal and confidential basis, with the aim of resolving problems as quickly as possible. However, the PALS service does not deal with formal complaints being pursued under the NHS complaints procedure.

There are also charities that assist people with complaints. The Patients Association investigates many different health and care concerns from patients, as well as monitoring trends in patient satisfaction and NHS targets, promoting good practice amongst healthcare professionals, supporting patients through unique casework, leading two UK parliamentary committees, and undertaking their own research.

Action against Medical Accidents is another charity, which provides free independent advice and support to people affected by medical accidents (lapses in patient safety) through their specialist helpline, written casework, and inquest support services. They also work in partnership with health professionals, the NHS, government departments, lawyers, and patients to improve patient safety and justice. They have a panel of lawyers, who specialise in compensation claims against health services providers.

Legal claims against the NHS and other healthcare providers should be handled by a lawyer. There is the issue of limitation i.e. time limits in such claims can be a complex one and so a referral should be made to a lawyer as soon as possible. Action against Medical Accidents has a panel of solicitors who specialise in what are known as 'clinical negligence' claims i.e. claims against healthcare providers.

Sometimes an apology or an appreciation that something has gone wrong can be enough to defuse a situation. Complainants have different objectives and sometimes that objective may be simply knowing that someone has listened and acknowledged that an error has been made.

6.6: The Local Authority Social Services and National Health Service Complaints (England) Regulations (2009)

These are the main regulations that govern most health services providers. It is important to realise that these regulations also cover 'independent providers', which means organisations providing NHS services as a private contractor. These private contractors are also covered by the complaints procedure. So, for instance, if a patient is treated in a private hospital paid for by the NHS, their complaint would be made under the NHS complaints procedure.

The Department of Health publishes a helpful guide to making a complaint, which can be found at: https://www.gov.uk/government/publications/the-nhs-constitution-for-england/how-do-i-give-feedback-or-make-a-complaint-about-an-nhs-service.

6.6.1: General rules for NHS complaints handling

Regulation 3 requires 'responsible bodies' (i.e. a NHS Trust or a GP practice) to make arrangements for the handling and consideration of complaints. The arrangements for dealing with complaints must be such as to ensure that:

- complaints are dealt with efficiently
- complaints are properly investigated
- complainants are treated with respect and courtesy
- complainants receive, so far as is reasonably practical:
    - assistance to enable them to understand the procedure in relation to complaints, or

- advice on where they may obtain such assistance
- complainants receive a timely and appropriate response
- complainants are told the outcome of the investigation of their complaint
- action is taken, if necessary, in the light of the outcome of a complaint.

6.6.2: Complaints managers and responsible persons

Regulation 4 sets out who deals with the complaint within the organisation. It says that each body must designate a responsible person for ensuring compliance with the complaints regulations. The responsible person should be the chief executive. Each body should also designate a complaints manager for overseeing complaints although this may be the chief executive.

6.6.3: Complaints not covered by the complaints system

Regulation 8 deals with those complaints that are not covered by the complaints system, which include matters that are with the Parliamentary and Health Service Ombudsman (PHSO) or complaints under the Freedom of Information Act (2000). Note that under the health services complaints system, a responsible body can investigate a complaint even if it is the subject of litigation, or it is proceeding through a tribunal.

However, as we will see below when we examine the role of the PHSO, S4 of the Health Commissioners Act (1993) (the main act that defines what the PHSO can do in relation to medical complaints) says that the PHSO shall not conduct an investigation where there are other legal avenues available. So, a complaint that goes through the medical healthcare complaints system, may be excluded by the PHSO because it could be pursued through other legal methods.

If there are other legal avenues available, then the help of a specialist lawyer will be required.

6.6.4: Duty to co-operate

Regulation 9 deals with the situation where two different bodies are concerned. Each must co-operate with the other. Regulation 11 deals with a complaint made to both an NHS body and a social care provider, i.e. a local authority. Again, each must co-operate with the other.

6.6.5: Time limits and time scales

Regulation 12 sets out the time limit for making a complaint. This is 12 months after the date of the event which gave rise to the complaint, or 12 months after the date on which it came to the notice of the complainant. The time limit can be waived if the complainant had good reasons for not making the complaint within that time limit and if, notwithstanding the delay, it is still possible to investigate the complaint effectively and fairly.

Regulation 13 sets out the time scales for processing the complaint. The responsible body dealing with the complaint has to acknowledge the complaint no later than 3 working days from receipt. At the time that it acknowledges the complaint, the responsible body must offer to discuss with the complainant (at a time to be agreed with the complainant) the manner in which the complaint is to be handled; the period within which the investigation of the complaint is likely to be completed; and when the response is likely to be sent to the complainant.

The complainant does not have to accept the offer of a discussion. If that happens then the responsible body can decide its response time itself and then notify the complainant in writing of that response time.

6.6.6: The investigation

Regulation 14 sets out the way in which the responsible body investigates and responds. During the investigation it must keep the complainant informed, as far as is reasonably practicable, as to the progress of the investigation. Then, after completion, it must send the complainant a response in writing, signed by the responsible person, which includes:

- An explanation of how the complaint has been considered.
- The conclusions reached about the complaint, including any matters specified in the complaint or for which the responsible body considers that remedial action is needed.
- Confirmation as to whether the responsible body is satisfied that any action needed has been taken or is proposed to be taken.
- Where the complaint relates wholly or in part to the functions of a local authority, details of the complainant's right to take their complaint to the Local Government and Social Care Ombudsman.
- Details of the complainant's right to take their complaint to the Parliamentary and Health Services Ombudsman.

The responsible body has six months in which to put together the response above. If it doesn't, then it must write to the complainant explaining why and get a response together as soon as possible.

Regulation 15 says that the complaint can be handled by email if the complainant and the responsible body agree. Regulation 16 requires the responsible body to publicise details of its complaints procedures on its website. Regulations 17 and 18 require that body to keep a record of those complaints and monitor them, as well as producing an annual report.

6.7: The NHS Bodies and Local Authorities (Partnership Arrangements, Care Trusts, Public Health and Local Healthwatch) Regulations (2012)

Local authorities provide services in conjunction with the NHS and other independent bodies. Part 5 of these regulations make provision for complaints about these kinds of services. This might be an elderly person who is receiving care from the local authority as well as medical treatment from the NHS.

Regulation 20 specifies the range of complaints that can made. Regulation 21 requires the local authority and the NHS service provider to make arrangements for the handling of complaints. Regulation 22 requires each to designate a person to be responsible for ensuring compliance with the arrangements and a complaints manager to be responsible for managing the complaints procedure.

Regulation 23 specifies the persons who may make complaints under these regulations and regulation 24 makes provision as to the circumstances in which each local authority/NHS service provider will have a duty to handle these complaints in. Regulation 25 specifies certain types of complaint which are not required to be dealt with in accordance with the regulations.

Regulation 26 makes provision for local authorities to co-operate in relation to complaints being considered by one local authority which also fall to be handled by another local authority.

Regulation 27 specifies the time limit for making a complaint and regulation 28 makes provision about how a complaint is to be made and processed initially, including determining the likely period for investigating and responding to the complaint. Regulation 29 provides for the investigation of the complaint and the response to the complainant. Regulation 30 makes provision for electronic communications.

Each responsible body must ensure that its complaints arrangements are made available to the public (Regulation 31); must maintain records for the purpose of monitoring complaints arrangements (Regulation 32); and must prepare and make available an annual report, although that report may form part of a wider report relating to other prescribed complaints procedures (Regulation 33).

6.8: Making a complaint about a health service professional

A person might wish to complain about a health service professional rather than their actual treatment. There are a series of organisations that regulate health services professionals. Each of these organisations sets out precisely what they can and cannot do for people who have concerns about health service professionals. It is important to study the information on these organisation's individual websites before making any kind of complaint. These regulatory bodies are set up to ensure that their members are acting professionally and they can discipline or remove a member if they act in the wrong way.

This means that when a complaint is made about a member, the regulatory body follows a disciplinary process against that member, which is different from the complaints process against the NHS or a private healthcare provider. Very briefly, the process will be as follows:

- When a person complains to a regulator via the forms available on its website or sent out to them on request, they are not involved in any disciplinary proceedings, save to the extent that they may be a witness.

- If a regulator thinks that the complaint discloses possible misconduct, deficient professional performance or impairment of fitness to practice by reason of health, then the professional is sent a copy of the complaint and any evidence the regulator decides to gather at that stage. The regulator may wish to ask the complainant for documents, consent to access their clinical notes, or even take a witness statement. Normally the complainant will be sent a copy of the professional's response to the complaint and asked to comment further.

- A decision-maker (case examiner or investigating committee) will then decide whether any action should be taken, which may involve giving advice or a warning to the professional, or referring them to a disciplinary tribunal.

- In the event that the matter goes to a disciplinary tribunal, the complainant may well be called to give oral evidence in a public hearing.

A number of professional regulatory bodies are set up under statute. There is a list together with the statutes/statutory orders that relate to them in S227(8) of the Health and Social Care Act (2012). These bodies all have their own complaints procedures.

The General Medical Council helps to protect patients and improve medical education and practice across the UK. It decides which doctors are qualified to work in the UK, and it oversees medical education and training. It also sets the standards that doctors need to follow, and makes sure that they continue to meet these standards throughout their careers. When a serious concern is raised about a doctor's behaviour, health or performance, they can investigate to see if the doctor is putting the safety of patients, or the public's confidence in doctors, at risk. Their website address is www.gmc-uk.org.

The General Dental Council is the regulator of both dentists and dental care professionals in the UK. Their primary purpose is to protect patient safety and maintain public confidence in dental services. They register qualified dental professionals, set standards of dental practice, investigate complaints about dental professionals' fitness to practice, and work to ensure the quality of dental education. Their website address is www.gdc-uk.org.

The General Optical Council is the regulator for the optical professions in the UK. They register optometrists, dispensing opticians, student opticians and optical businesses. They set standards for education and training, performance and conduct, approve qualifications leading to registration, maintain a register of individuals who are qualified and fit to practice, and investigate where registrants' fitness to practice or carry on business is impaired. Their website address is www.optical.org.

The General Osteopathic Council regulates the practice of osteopathy in the UK. They work with the public and osteopathic profession to promote patient safety by registering qualified professionals, and setting, maintaining and developing standards of osteopathic practice and conduct. They also deal with concerns and complaints about osteopaths. Their website address is www.osteopathy.org.uk.

The General Chiropractic Council regulates chiropractors in the UK to ensure the safety of patients undergoing chiropractic treatment. They protect the health and safety of the public by ensuring high standards of practice in the chiropractic profession. They also have the power to deal with chiropractors whose fitness to practice is called into question. Their website is www.gcc-uk.org.

The General Pharmaceutical Council protects, promotes and maintains the health and safety of people who use services from pharmacy professionals or from registered pharmacies. They investigate concerns about pharmacists and pharmacy technicians that could suggest there is a risk to patient safety or could affect the public's confidence in pharmacy. Their website address is www.pharmacyregulation.org.

The Nursing and Midwifery Council regulates nurses and midwives and sets standards of education, training, conduct and performance. They maintain a register of nurses and midwives allowed to practice in the UK, and they ensure that their members keep their skills and knowledge up to date and uphold their professional standards. Their website address is www.nmc.org.uk.

The Health and Care Professions Council (HCPC) regulates a number of different professions, all of which have titles that are protected by law. This means, for example, that anyone using the titles 'physiotherapist' or 'dietitian' has to be registered with them. Currently they regulate the following professions:

- Arts therapists.
- Biomedical scientists.
- Chiropodists/podiatrists.
- Clinical scientists.
- Dietitians.
- Hearing aid dispensers.
- Occupational therapists.
- Operating department practitioners.
- Orthoptists.
- Paramedics.
- Physiotherapists.
- Practitioner psychologists.
- Prosthetists.
- Orthotists.
- Radiographers.
- Social workers in England.
- Speech and language therapists.

So, if a person has a concern about one of these professionals, they can contact the HCPC to report that concern. Their website can be found at: www.hcpc-uk.co.uk.

Under the Children and Social Work Act (2017), social workers in England will be regulated by a new body, Social Work England, in the future instead of by the HCPC. The HCPC's website states that it does not expect Social Work England to begin regulating social workers before Spring 2019.

We also have the Professional Standards Authority for Health and Social Care. This authority reviews the work of the regulators of health and care professionals, such as the HCPC. However, they also accredit organisations that register health and care practitioners in unregulated occupations. They have a list of associations who are accredited with them: http://www.professionalstandards.org.uk/what-we-do/accredited-registers/find-a-register.

One of these is the British Association for Counselling and Psychotherapy: www.bacp.co.uk. This is described as a membership organisation and a registered charity, which sets standards for therapeutic practice and provides information for therapists, clients of therapy, and the general public. It also provides a complaints procedure.

Another organisation is Save Face: www.saveface.co.uk, which operates a register for doctors, nurses and dentists who provide non-surgical cosmetic treatments. They work in clinics that have been inspected and verified to meet Save Face's standards. They also provide their own complaints procedure.

These bodies tend to have a disciplinary process similar to the statutory regulators mentioned above, such as the General Medical Council. However, there is a key distinction. If a person practices in an area, where the regulation is carried out by a voluntary membership-based organisation (rather than an organisation established by statute such as the General Medical Council), then there is nothing to stop them from carrying on in that area, whether they are recognised by the membership organisation or not, or indeed even after they have been expelled from that organisation. This is why some healthcare practitioners need to be carefully checked out.

6.9: Private sector health service providers

Privately funded health services are regulated under the Care Standards Act (2000) and what is now the Care Quality Commission.

Private health is not covered by the Local Authority Social Services and National Health Service Complaints (England) Regulations (2009) – unless they are paid for by the NHS or in circumstances where an NHS health services provider is paid privately. Moreover, the Parliamentary and Health Service Ombudsman cannot look into complaints about privately-funded healthcare services.

The complaint has to be directed to the private health service provider. Regulation 23 of the Private and Voluntary Healthcare (England) Regulations (2001) requires independent providers to establish a complaints procedure. Consequently, it is important to establish the identity of that provider and find their procedure.

The Independent Sector Complaints Adjudication Service (ISCAS) provides independent adjudication on complaints about ISCAS members. It has produced a patients' guide with input from the Patients Association, which explains how to make a complaint about an ISCAS member using the ISCAS complaints code of practice. Their website address is: www.iscas.org.uk/patients-complaints-process.

There is also the Independent Healthcare Advisory Services, a trade organization that represents over 250 hospitals that provide services to insured, self-paying and NHS-funded patients. They have published a guide entitled *Making a Complaint in the Independent Sector*, which can be found at: www.privatehealth.co.uk/.../IHAS-Making-Complaints-A-Guide-For-Patients.pdf.

6.10: Mental Health

The rising incidence of dementia in the elderly has created an increasing need for the representation of those who lack mental capacity. At the same time, the government has introduced legislation to help those in psychiatric institutions.

A person detained by a psychiatric hospital has the right to challenge that detention before a mental health tribunal. This is a subject beyond the scope of this book, and would need input from a specialist lawyer. A person can also complain about a psychiatric hospital or psychiatric treatment using the NHS and private healthcare procedures described above.

6.10.1: Independent Mental Capacity Advocates (IMCAs)

S35 to S41 of the Mental Capacity Act (2005) created a scheme to provide an independent mental capacity advocate where certain decisions need to be taken for particularly vulnerable people (aged 16 or over) who lack capacity. This may include older people with dementia who have lost contact with all friends and family, or people with severe learning disabilities or long term mental health problems, who have been in residential institutions for long periods and lack outside contacts. Such people are given representation and provided with support when decisions are to be made about serious medical treatment or significant changes of residence provided by public bodies. An IMCA must be allocated, and then consulted, for people lacking capacity who have no-one else to support them.

The 2005 act also has a code of practice published by the government. Chapter 10 of that code contains an explanation of what IMCA's do: https://www.gov.uk/government/uploads/system/uploads/attachment_data/file/497253/Mental-capacity-act-code-of-practice.pdf

S35(1) of the 2005 act obliges the local authority to make such arrangements as it considers reasonable to enable IMCAs to be available for representing and supporting persons, where the following acts or decisions are proposed for them:

- Serious medical treatment by the NHS.
- Accommodation by the NHS.
- Accommodation by a local authority.
- Detention in a hospital or care home for the purposes of treatment.

The 2005 act is accompanied by the Mental Capacity Act (2005) (Independent Mental Capacity Advocates) (General) Regulations (2006), which define 'serious medical treatment'. The regulations also sets out who can be appointed to act as an IMCA and describes the IMCA's functions once they have been instructed to represent a person in a particular case.

A further set of regulations, the Mental Capacity Act (2005) (Independent Mental Capacity Advocates) (Expansion of Role) Regulations (2006), gives a local authority a discretionary powers to provide an IMCA for a person without capacity in other circumstances. One of those sets of circumstances is set out in regulation 4, where it is alleged that the person without capacity is or has been abused or neglected by another person or that they are abusing or have abused another person.

Local authorities and the NHS have been issued with Department of Health guidance on this issue entitled *No Secrets: Guidance on developing and implementing multi-agency policies and procedures to protect vulnerable adults from abuse*: https://www.gov.uk/government/publications/no-secrets-guidance-on-protecting-vulnerable-adults-in-care.

6.10.2: Independent Mental Health Advocates (IMHAs)

S130A of the Mental Health Act (1983) obliges a local authority to provide help to 'qualifying patients' by offering them IMHA's. A 'qualifying patient' is either an adult or a child, who is likely to be detained in a psychiatric hospital under the Mental Health Act (1983) or who is put under the protection of a guardian, or classed as a community patient (i.e. a patient being treated in the community) under the 1983 act. It can also include adults and children who are discussing psychiatric treatment with a doctor.

The 1983 act is accompanied by the Mental Health Act (1983) (Independent Mental Health Advocates) (England) Regulations (2008). These set out the circumstances in which a person may be appointed to be an IMHA. Regulation 6 provides that a person can only act as an IMHA if they have satisfied certain requirements as to experience, training, good character and independence. That regulation also provides that in deciding whether to appoint a person to act as an IMHA, regard is to be had to guidance issued by the government.

That guidance can be found in a code of practice issued under the Mental Health Act (1983). The section on IMHA's can be found at Chapter 6 of that guidance: https://www.gov.uk/government/uploads/system/uploads/attachment_data/file/435512/MHA_Code_of_Practice.PDF.

6.11: The Parliamentary and Health Service Ombudsman (PHSO)

As we saw in Chapter 3, the Draft Public Service Ombudsman Act will merge the Local Government and Social Care Ombudsman and the Parliamentary and Health Service Ombudsman (PHSO) and bring them into one office, the Public Service Ombudsman. Where a complainant cannot achieve resolution via the NHS complaints procedure, that complainant can apply to the PHSO.

The PHSO is effectively a merger of the office of the Parliamentary Commissioner and the Health Commissioner. Commissioner is the term used by the legislation to describe an Ombudsman. As we will see below, and in other chapters of this book, the Parliamentary Commissioner investigates government departments. In this and other chapters, we use the term PHSO to mean both types of commissioner.

As we saw with the Local Government and Social Care Ombudsman, complaints that could be taken forward by way of other legal methods, are excluded from the PHSO's remit.

S4 of the Health Commissioners Act (1993) (the main act that defines what the PHSO can do in relation to medical complaints) says that the PHSO shall not conduct an investigation in respect of action in relation to which the person aggrieved has or had a right of appeal, reference or review to or before a tribunal (i.e. mental health tribunal) or a remedy by way of proceedings in any court of law. Consequently, other legal avenues are excluded from the remit of the PHSO. The PHSO may deal with the complaint if it is satisfied that in the particular circumstances it is not reasonable to expect that person to resort or have resorted to that other legal venue.

S8(1) of the Health Commissioners Act (1993) (the main act that defines what the PHSO can do in relation to medical complaints) says that a complaint may be made by an individual or a body of persons, whether incorporated or not (i.e. a limited company or association of people) but not a public authority such as a local authority.

S9(2) says that the complaint must be brought in writing. S9(3) says that the complaint must be brought by the person 'aggrieved' i.e. affected, or it can be brought by a representative, a member of his family, or 'some body or individual suitable to represent him'.

There is a time limit of one year from the date the complainant first knew about the matters alleged in the complaint. Section 9(4) of the 1993 act says that the PHSO will not entertain the complaint if it is made more than a year after the day on which the complainant 'first had notice of the matters alleged in the complaint' unless the PHSO considers it 'reasonable' to do so.

S10 says that a 'health body' i.e. an NHS trust can refer a complaint to the PHSO. Once the PHSO receives a complaint and it decides that it can deal with it, then it will commence an investigation. The subject of the complaint, the health body, is required to co-operate and provide the necessary evidence. At the conclusion of the investigation, the PHSO will produce a report which will be sent to the complainant and the health body.

S18ZA says that the PHSO can work with the Local Government and Social Care Ombudsman if need be. S18A says that the PHSO can also give information to the Information Commissioner (see Chapter 12). This might be where the PHSO discovers a serious breach of data protection laws, i.e. someone's confidential medical notes being disclosed inadvertently.

The PHSO's website can be found at: www.ombudsman.org.uk. The PHSO covers a wide range of government activities as well as the NHS. They also cover a number of UK government departments and other UK public organisations, such as the benefits system (see Chapter 9), the Crown Prosecution Service (see Chapter 10) and in certain circumstances decisions taken by the Prisons and Probation Ombudsman. A list of these organisations can be found at: www.ombudsman.org.uk/making-complaint/what-we-can-and-cant-help/government-organisations-we-can-investigate.

The PHSO also publishes a series of principles (one of which we saw in Chapter 3) which are used to guide and inform other types of Ombudsmen as well as bodies such as the Independent Office for Police Conduct (see Chapter 10):

- Principles of good administration.
- Principles of good complaint handling.
- Principles for remedy.

These principles can be found at: www.ombudsman.org.uk/about-us/our-principles.

6.12: Key points

- The Care Quality Commission (CQC) is the independent regulator for health and social care in England.
- The Health and Social Care Act (2008) sets out who has to be registered with the CQC and the fundamental health and safety standards for healthcare providers.
- The Health and Social Care Act (2012) sets out the current structure of the NHS. This is a complex structure which consists of several bodies. It is important to identify the right one.
- Independent advocacy may be available, funded by local authorities, for complaints against the NHS.
- S114 of the Health and Social Care (Community Health and Standards) Act 2003 requires the NHS to have a complaints system.
- The Local Authority Social Services and National Health Services Complaints (England) Regulations (2009) sets out the actual complaints procedure.
- Healthcare providers have a duty to cooperate with one another when handling complaints.
- Complaints should be brought within 12 months and should generally be completed within six months.

- Complainants can take their complaint to the Parliamentary and Health Services Ombudsman. There is a time limit of 12 months, but this can be extended.
- Complaints against health services professionals should be made to the appropriate body.
- The NHS complaints procedure does not cover private healthcare.

6.13: Case summaries

The PHSO publishes summaries of cases they have investigated on their website. It can be found at: https://www.ombudsman.org.uk/about-us/how-our-casework-makes-difference/case-summaries?page=0.

GP failed to take patient's mental health symptoms into account when treating him

https://www.ombudsman.org.uk/about-us/how-our-casework-makes-difference/case-summaries/881

Mr K saw his GP several times over many months about his painful foot and blocked nose. His mental health issues were known to the GP but Mr K felt that his GP was always rushed and did not take his mental health problems into account when treating him.

The PHSO found that the GP's examinations and record keeping were not in accordance with General Medical Council guidelines. It found that it had treated Mr K's mental health conditions appropriately by referring him for psychiatric services but did not consider the distress that his failure to promptly investigate the foot and nose symptoms caused to Mr K.

After the PHSO investigation the GP acknowledged and apologised for the failings and paid Mr K £1000 in recognition of the distress and inconvenience caused.

Clinical Commissioning Group (CCG) unreasonably refused to fund IVF

https://www.ombudsman.org.uk/about-us/how-our-casework-makes-difference/case-summaries/959

Following a road traffic accident, Mr A had suffered injuries to his spinal cord. His GP had suggested he seek fertility treatment. Mr A and Ms B applied for NHS funding for IVF on three occasions and each time the CCG declined. The PHSO found that the CCG had failed to show that it had considered Mr A's exceptional circumstances. The CCG had not included the basis for its decision in its records or decision letters. After the PHSO investigation, the CCG reconsidered its decision. It declined funding again but provided evidence to support its new decision.

Nursing staff did not monitor older patient, who then developed pressure sore

https://www.ombudsman.org.uk/about-us/how-our-casework-makes-difference/case-summaries/539

Mr D complained that his mother, Mrs G, was not adequately monitored while she was in hospital. Although the trust had acknowledged some failings the PHSO found that:

- Mrs G did not receive adequate care
- the inadequate care did, on the balance of probabilities, lead to her developing avoidable pressure sores
- the record keeping of Mrs G's condition was poor.

After the PHSO investigation the trust acknowledged and apologised for its failings and paid Mrs G £750 to recognise the avoidable pressure sores she developed.

Hospital missed opportunities to save man's sight

https://www.ombudsman.org.uk/about-us/how-our-casework-makes-difference/case-summaries/1059

Mr G suffered eye pain a few days after undergoing eye surgery. An ophthalmologist treated Mr G with medication to reduce the pressure in his eye but discharged him before there was any evidence the treatment had worked. Mr G returned, as advised, after 4 days and was referred to a glaucoma specialist for specialist treatment however this treatment was not successful and he lost the sight in his eye.

The PHSO found that Mr G should have been given more aggressive treatment and should not have been discharged until his eye pressure had reduced. Following the PHSO investigation the trust apologised to Mr G, paid him £5000 compensation and explained what actions it would take to prevent this happening again.

Possible missed opportunity to prevent suicide

https://www.ombudsman.org.uk/about-us/how-our-casework-makes-difference/case-summaries/1060

Miss J had a history of depression and took an overdose. She was briefly admitted to the trust but, as she preferred to be cared for by her family, was discharged home under the crisis and home treatment team ('the crisis team'). Three weeks later she took a second overdose. She was again discharged under the care of the crisis team. A few days later she was readmitted and then allowed home with medication. A few more days later Miss J was readmitted to hospital after making a further suicide attempt. The trust reassessed her, a few days after this, as having a 'low' risk of self-harm – Miss J hanged herself within the next two days.

The PHSO found that, although Miss J was prescribed medication in line with recognised standards, the trust's risk assessments and the way it managed her care were not reasonable. The trust apologised to the family and paid them £2500 in recognition of the distress caused.

GP practice missed opportunity to prevent patient from having a fatal pulmonary embolism

https://www.ombudsman.org.uk/about-us/how-our-casework-makes-difference/case-summaries/1048

Mrs H, in her early fifties, saw her GP about pain and swelling in her leg and was prescribed painkillers. A few days later, still in pain, she saw a second GP who again prescribed painkillers. Nine days later she was admitted to hospital where she had a pulmonary embolism and died. The PHSO found that the GP practice had missed two opportunities to arrange urgent care, which very likely would have avoided Mrs H's fatal pulmonary embolism.

The trust apologised to Mr H and paid him £15,000. The trust also put in place more tests for deep vein thrombosis (DVT) and reported to the PHSO that it had subsequently found DVT in patients where it had not expected to.

there are some grammar, foundation and voluntary schools which are maintained by a local authority and others that are independent schools.

The New Schools Network has published a guide – *Comparison of Different Types of School: A guide to schools in England October 2016*, which is very helpful. There is also the government guide - www.gov.uk/types-of-school/overview.

The most common types of schools are:

- community schools, maintained by the local authority
- foundation schools and voluntary schools, which have more freedom to change the way they do things than community schools
- academies, run by a governing body, independent from the local authority – they can follow a different curriculum
- grammar schools – run by the local authority, a foundation body or a trust – they select all or most of their pupils based on academic ability.

There are then other types of schools. Faith schools have to follow the national curriculum but they can choose what they teach in religious studies. They may have different admissions criteria and staffing policies to state schools.

Free schools are funded by the government but are free from local authority control and are independent schools. They cannot use academic selection processes like a grammar school but can set their own pay and conditions for staff, as well as changing the length of school terms and the school day. They do not have to follow the national curriculum.

Private schools are independent schools. They charge fees to attend rather than being funded by the government. They have their own governing bodies, which set the admissions policy and employ staff. Most private schools are funded by fees, gifts and endowments. They are less heavily regulated than maintained schools.

Academies are also independent schools, funded by the government and other sponsors such as businesses and charities. They do not have to follow the national curriculum and can set their own term times. However, they still have to follow the same rules on admissions, special educational needs, and exclusions as other state schools.

City technology colleges are independent schools in urban areas, which are owned and funded by companies as well as central government. They have a particular emphasis on technological and practical skills.

State boarding schools provide free education but charge fees for boarding. Some state boarding schools are run by local councils and some are run as academies or free schools. They provide for children who have a particular need to board and will assess children's suitability for boarding.

Special schools teach pupils aged 11 and older with special educational needs. They can be either maintained or non-maintained.

7.3: State or maintained schools

S29 of the Education Act (2002) states that the governing body of a maintained school must establish procedures for dealing with all complaints relating to the school. The governing body is also required to publicise their procedures and have regard to any guidance given from time to time by the Department of Education.

7.3.1: Complaints guidance for state schools

The present guidance is contained in *Best Practice Advice for School Complaints Procedures 2016: Departmental advice for maintained schools, maintained nursery schools and local authorities* published by the Department of Education. This can be found at: https://www.gov.uk/government/publications/school-complaints-procedures.

This guidance makes it clear that the school's complaints procedure will not apply to exclusions, admissions, assessment of special educational needs, school re-organisation, child protection investigations, staff grievances, whistleblowing, or disciplinary procedures, which are beyond the scope of this book.

Consequently the guidance would apply to issues such as discrimination and bullying. It would also apply to financial support for individual pupils, particularly for those in care, who are sometimes entitled to pupil premiums. The writers have experienced cases where pupil premium money is put into a central 'pot' and not utilised for the benefit of the respective child.

The guidance begins by distinguishing between a complaint and a concern, so it encourages complainants and the school to try and settle the matter without using the formal procedure. Any person, including members of the general public, may make a complaint about any facilities or services that a school provides. Schools must not limit complaints to parents or carers of children who are registered at the school.

7.3.2: The complaints procedure for maintained schools

Each local authority will have a model procedure for their schools but the guidance says that schools can tailor their complaints procedure to their own circumstances. It also recommends that the governing body of the school ensures that any third party providers offering community facilities or services through the school premises, or using school facilities, have their own complaints procedure in place. This could be, for instance, private companies providing sports coaching or outside activities. These outside bodies are not covered by the school's complaints procedure.

The guidance tells governing bodies to be 'mindful' of the language used in the complaints procedure. It recommends that schools say what they 'will' do rather than what they 'should' or 'may' do. The reason for this is that, where a policy states that a school 'should' do something which they then choose not to do, and the matter is then taken to the Department for Education, the school may be asked to provide a written explanation for the reasons why they deviated from best practice. Other 'tips' for best practice are:

- The complainant should be asked at the earliest stage what they think might resolve the issue.

- The complaints procedure should set out the steps to follow in the event that the head teacher or member of the governing body is the subject of the complaint. Complaints against the head teacher are usually first dealt with by the Chair of Governors. Complaints against the Chair of Governors or any individual governor should be made by writing to the Clerk to the Governing Body.

- The procedure should be easily accessible, publicised, simple to understand and use, impartial, and finally non-adversarial (which means that it should not be a litigation process).

- There should be a full and fair investigation by an independent person where necessary.

- The complaint should be kept confidential insofar as possible.

- All the points at issue should be addressed. An effective response and, where appropriate, redress should be provided.

- The procedure should provide information to the school's senior management team so that services can be improved. The Guidance recommends review of the complaints procedure every two to three years.

- The response to the complaint should be timely and realistic. Reasonable time limits for each action should be set within each stage and, where further investigations are necessary; the procedure should set new time limits; send the complainant details of any new deadlines; and give an explanation for the delay.

- Schools are entitled to expect complaints to be made as soon as possible after an incident arises (three months is generally considered to be an acceptable time frame in which to lodge a complaint).

- Schools should ensure that, if their policy includes a cut-off timeframe, they will consider exceptions. This should be reflected in their procedures.

- Schools are free to choose how many stages their procedure will include – two or three formal school-based stages are likely to be sufficient for most schools.

- Determining what the appeal panel considers is for the school to decide.

- The complaints procedure must not suggest that a complaint can only be escalated to the next stage if the school permits it. Regardless of how many stages the school chooses to operate, or whether or not the complaint is 'justified', a dissatisfied complainant must always be given the opportunity to complete the complaints procedure in full.

- Some procedures may also allow for an additional stage if the local authority, diocese (if the school is run by the church), or other external agency provides an independent appeal or review.

7.3.3: Other features of the maintained schools complaints procedure

The guidance also states that schools must ensure that they comply with their obligations under the Equality Act (2010). This means that they have to allow for complainants with disabilities or learning difficulties. A complaint may be made in person, by telephone, or in writing, and brief records should be kept of the complaint and its progress through the procedure.

Complaints should not be shared with the whole governing body, except in very general terms, in case an appeal panel needs to be formed out of that same governing body. The idea here is that if the governing body has already discussed the complaint, then it would make it more difficult for them to be impartial if they have to consider it themselves. However, there are situations where the whole governing body will be aware of the substance of a complaint before the final stage has been completed. In those circumstances, schools should arrange for an independent panel to hear the complaint. They may approach a different school to ask for help or the local governor services team at the local authority or the diocese. Complainants actually have the right to request an independent panel, if they believe there is likely to be bias in the proceedings. Schools should consider the request but, ultimately, the decision is made by the governors.

Finally, schools can refuse to deal with complaints from serial or persistent complainants, although they have to take care when exercising that right, and they should have a policy in place to deal with those circumstances.

7.3.4: The role of the school complaints unit

If a complainant has completed the schools' procedures and remains dissatisfied, they have the right to refer their complaint to the Department of Education, which has a duty to consider all complaints raised. The School Complaints Unit (SCU) considers complaints relating to local authority maintained schools in England. It will look at whether the school followed its own complaints policy and any other relevant statutory policies. However the SCU is limited in what it can do. It will only intervene where the governing body has acted unlawfully or unreasonably and where it is expedient or practical to do so. However the SCU will not normally re-investigate the substance of the complaint and it will not overturn a school's decision about a complaint, except in exceptional circumstances where it is clear the school has acted unlawfully or unreasonably. If the SCU finds that the school has not handled a complaint in accordance with its procedure, it may request that the complaint is looked at again.

If legislative or policy breaches are found, the SCU will report them to the school and the complainant and, where necessary, ask for corrective action to be taken. The SCU normally also seeks written assurances as to future conduct. Failure to carry out remedial actions or provide written assurances could ultimately result in a formal direction being issued by the Department of Education in accordance with her powers under sections 496 and 497 of the Education Act (1996). The SCU have a National Helpline: 0370 000 2288 and a website: www.education.gov.uk/help/contactus. Their address is Department for Education School Complaints Unit, 2nd Floor, Piccadilly Gate Store Street, Manchester, M1 2WD.

7.3.5: Complaining to Ofsted about 'whole school' issues

There is a right to complain to Ofsted about maintained schools. These include community, foundation and voluntary schools and maintained nursery schools as well as academies, city technology colleges, city colleges for the technology of the arts, and non-maintained special schools. The issues about which the complaint can be made are limited. The complaint has to be about something that affects the whole school, not just one individual pupil. The Education (Investigation of Parents' Complaints) (England) Regulations (2007) set out those issues, which are:

- the quality of the education provided in the school
- how far the education provided in the school meets the needs of the range of pupils at the school
- the educational standards achieved in the school
- the quality of the leadership in and management of the school, including whether the financial resources made available to the school are managed effectively
- the spiritual, moral, social and cultural development of the pupils at the school
- the contribution made by the school to the well-being of those pupils
- the contribution made by the school to community cohesion.

Ofsted publish guidance for parents *Complaints to Ofsted about Schools* which can be found at: www.gov.uk/government/publications/complaints-to-ofsted-about-schools-guidance-for-parents.

Ofsted will not investigate cases that involve:

- admission procedures
- pupil exclusions
- special educational needs
- religious education or the religious character of a school
- changes to the curriculum
- incidents that have taken place in the school
- the way in which a school investigated or responded to a complaint.

The complaint must be raised with the school first under their own procedures. Thereafter, the complainant can take their complaint direct to Ofsted using their online complaints form: www.ofsted.gov.uk/onlinecomplaints. Ofsted have a number of options open to them. They may take no further action, forward a copy of the complaint to their inspection team at the school's next inspection, bring forward an inspection or arrange immediate inspection if the concerns are very serious. Alternatively, they can send any concerns about child protection to social services or the police.

7.4: Complaints about independent schools

All independent schools must be registered with the government and are inspected regularly. Half of them are inspected by Ofsted. The Independent Schools Inspectorate inspects schools that are members of the Independent Schools Council and some other schools are inspected by the School Inspection Service.

The Education (Independent School Standards) Regulations (2014) set out the standards by which independent educational institutions will be inspected. Those standards include the requirement to have a complaints procedure. The essential features of that complaints procedure are described in Part 7 of the schedule to the 2014 regulations:

- It must set out clear timescales for every stage.
- It must allow for a complaint to be initially made and considered on an informal basis.
- If the complainants are not satisfied with the informal approach, the school should make provision for the complaint to be made in writing.
- If the complainants wish the matter to be considered further, the procedure should make provision for a hearing before a panel of at least three people, who were not directly involved in previous consideration of the complaint.
- Where a panel hearing is convened, one person on the panel must be independent of the management and running of the school.
- Parents must be allowed to attend and be accompanied to a panel hearing if they wish.
- It must provide for the panel to make findings and recommendations and ensure that the complainant, proprietors, head teachers, and, where relevant, the person complained about, are given a copy of any findings and recommendations.
- Written records must be kept of all complaints and their outcomes.
- All correspondence, statements and records of complaints must be kept confidential but must be shown to the Independent Schools Inspectorate when they inspect.

Advice about complaining about a private school can be obtained from the Independent Schools Inspectorate. Their contact details are concerns@isi.net, Telephone: 020 7710 9900, Independent School Inspectorate, CAP House, 9-12 Long Lane, London, EC1A 9HA.

The Department for Education cannot investigate individual complaints about private, independent or non-maintained schools but it does have certain powers as a regulator if the school is not meeting standards set by the Department. It may consider any reports of failure to meet those standards and can arrange emergency inspection to look at pupil welfare and health and safety and make sure that serious failings are dealt with. It can also ask school inspectorates to take any minor failings into account when the school is next inspected.

Academies are regulated by the Education and Skills Funding Agency (ESFA). A complainant who has gone through an Academy's complaints procedure, but who is dissatisfied with the outcome, can write to the ESFA. The ESFA will not usually investigate complaints until the academy's own complaints procedure, including any hearing, has been exhausted. The ESFA's website can be found at: www.gov.uk/government/organisations/education-funding-agency/about/complaints-procedure.

7.5: Complaints about non-maintained special schools

There are schools approved by the Department for Education under Section 342 of the Education Act (1996) as independent special schools, to teach children with disabilities. They are non-profit making and they have to show that they operate to a level at least equivalent to state-maintained special schools.

The Non-Maintained Special Schools (England) Regulations (2015) make provision for the approval of non-maintained special schools and set out the requirements which must be met for a school to continue to be approved. The proprietor of the school must make arrangements for a complaints procedure, which:

- Is in writing.
- Is made available to registered pupils, parents of pupils, parents of prospective pupils, and members of staff, including supply staff.
- Sets out clear time scales for the management of a complaint.

- Allows for a complaint to be made and considered initially on an informal basis.

- Where a complainant is not satisfied with the response to an informal complaint, establishes a formal procedure for the complaint to be made in writing.

- Where a complainant is not satisfied with the response to the written complaint, makes provision for a hearing before an independent person appointed by or on behalf of the proprietor. That person cannot have been a governor of the school, or a member of staff, or member of supply staff, at the school; or the parent of a registered pupil, or former registered pupil, at the school; and cannot have been directly involved in any matter detailed in the complaint. The complainant should also be allowed to attend and be accompanied at such a hearing if they wish.

- Provides for the independent person to make findings and recommendations and stipulates that a copy of those findings and recommendations is provided to the complainant and, where relevant, the person complained about. The findings should also be available for inspection on the school premises by the proprietor and the head teacher.

- Provides for a written record to be kept of all complaints whether they are resolved following a formal procedure, or proceed to a hearing. There should be a record of the action taken by the school as a result of those complaints (regardless of whether they are upheld).

- Provides that correspondence, statements and records relating to individual complaints are to be kept confidential except where the Department for Education or HM Inspector of Schools request access to them.

7.6: Complaints about higher education and universities

Part 2 of the Higher Education Act (2004) introduced a statutory scheme for the review of complaints made by students or former students at qualifying institutions or by students working towards the grant of one of the qualifying institution's awards. It did this by setting up the office of the Office of the Independent Adjudicator (OIA) to administer a complaints scheme for students attending universities. From the outset, all universities in England were required to subscribe to this scheme, which now also covers colleges and other providers of higher education, and providers of school-centred initial teacher training. The OIA has a register of qualifying members on its website: www.oiahe.org.uk.

A student making a complaint against a qualifying institution must first exhaust that institution's complaints procedure. The recommended structure of that internal procedure can be found on the OIA's website and it is entitled *The Good Practice Framework: Handling student complaints and academic appeals*, which in turn draws on guidance issued by the Ombudsman Association.

Once the internal procedure is concluded, the institution must issue a 'completion of procedures letter' promptly and always within 28 days. The complainant then has a maximum of 12 months to bring their complaint to the OIA.

Under S15 of the 2004 act, each institution has to comply with any obligation placed on it by the OIA when reviewing a 'qualifying complaint'. The procedure by which the OIA reviews complaints is set out in Schedule 1 to 4 of the 2004 act. The OIA will only review complaints made by:

- a student or former student at that institution
- a student or former student at another institution (whether or not a qualifying institution) undertaking a course of study, or programme of research, leading to the grant of one of the qualifying institution's awards.

Certain types of complaint are excluded from the scheme. Examples are admissions, academic judgment, student employment, matters before a court or tribunal, any matters that have not had a material effect on the complainant, and matters previously considered by another alternative dispute resolution entity. The OIA may also decline to accept a complaint where it considers that the substantive event complained about occurred more than three years before the complaint form was received by the OIA, if it considers that to accept the complaint would seriously impair the effective operation of its scheme.

7.7: Complaints about apprenticeships

All organisations that deliver government funded apprenticeship training have to register with United Kingdom Register of Learning Providers and enter into a contract with the Education and Skills Funding Agency (see previously), which maintains a register of apprenticeship training providers. The organisation must be able to show that their apprentice has an apprenticeship agreement at the start of, and throughout, their apprenticeship between the employer and apprentice as defined in the Apprenticeships, Skills, Children and Learning Act (2009). The apprentice is required to sign an agreement with the employer, which will give that apprentice certain contractual and employment rights and protections, including the use of a grievance procedure.

If an apprentice has a complaint against his employer, then he would normally make use of the procedures contained in his contract of employment. However he could also bring his concerns to the attention of the ESFA, or to Ofsted, who have the right to inspect apprenticeships, where they concern children and young people.

7.8: Key points

- There are a number of different types of educational establishment in England, and their complaints procedures vary. Consequently, it is important to know the type of school against which the complaint is to be made.

- There is no Ombudsman for education in England. A complaint is generally made to the educational establishment itself, which will be obliged to have a complaints procedure, with a very limited right to complain to the Department for Education or some other body, depending on the type of educational establishment.

- The School Complaints Unit (SCU) considers complaints relating to local authority maintained schools in England.

- All types of schools are required to have some kind of complaints procedure and publish that procedure.

- The Education (Independent School Standards) Regulations (2014) set out the standards by which independent educational institutions will be inspected. Those standards include the requirement to have a complaints procedure.

- Higher education and universities are required to have a complaints procedure.

- There is no statutory complaints scheme for apprenticeships but apprentices may be able to make use of grievance procedures in their contracts. Government funded apprenticeships are subject to the oversight of the Education and Skills Funding Agency.

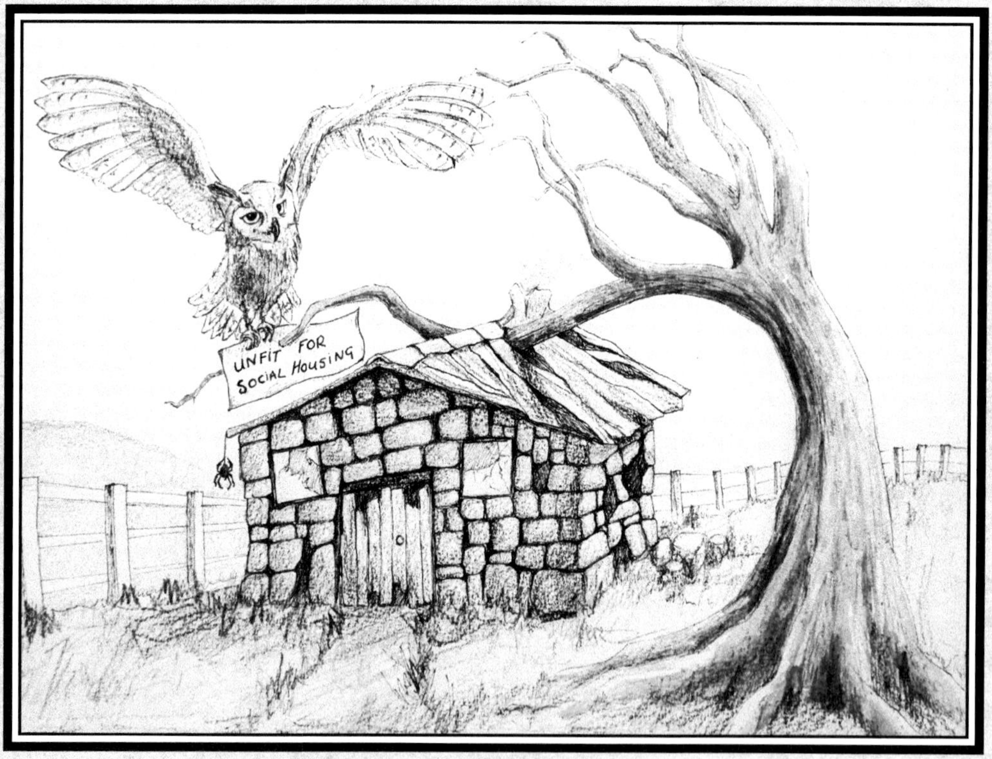
UNFIT FOR
SOCIAL HOUSING

Chapter 8: Complaints about housing issues and planning

8.1: The scheme for housing complaints

S51 and Schedule 2 of the Housing Act (1996) set up a scheme for tenants to make complaints about landlords of social housing. Social housing includes low cost rental properties (such as affordable rent properties) and low cost home ownership. Registered providers of social housing include both local authority landlords and private providers (such as not-for-profit housing associations and for-profit organisations). As with social care for children and adults, this scheme is subject to the Housing Ombudsman. Details of the scheme can be found on the Housing Ombudsman's website at: http://www.housing-ombudsman.org.uk.

The 1996 act requires social landlords to be members of the scheme. In this chapter from this point on, we refer to social landlords as 'members'. They pay an annual subscription dependent on the number of properties that they let. Other kinds of landlords can join the scheme on a voluntary basis.

As a condition of membership of the scheme, a member must:

- agree to be bound by the scheme
- establish and maintain a complaints procedure
- as part of that procedure, inform complainants of their right to bring complaints to the Housing Ombudsman under the scheme
- publish its complaints procedure and its membership of the scheme.

8.2: Who can complain and what can they complain about?

The following people can make a complaint:

- Tenants.
- An applicant for a property owned or managed by a member.
- A representative of a complainant, who is duly authorised by that complainant.
- A representative of a complainant who does not have the capacity to authorise a representative to act on their behalf.

A complaint has to be about the 'actions or omissions of a member' in connection with its housing activities. The person complaining, or on whose behalf a complaint is made, must have been adversely affected by something that the landlord has or not has done.

It is important to realise that housing issues go very wide and some issues are dealt with by the Local Government and Social Care Ombudsman, for instance homelessness and housing allocation. The Housing Ombudsman publishes a list of what is covered by its office and the Local Government and Social Care Ombudsman on its website under the heading 'Which Ombudsman for social housing complaints?': http://www.housing-ombudsman.org.uk/learning-faqs/factsheets/what-kind-of-complaints-can-we-consider/

The following cannot be the subject of a complaint:

- Complaints that are not brought to the attention of the member as a formal complaint within a reasonable period – this would normally be within 6 months of the matters arising.
- Complaints that concern policies, which have been properly decided by the member in accordance with relevant and appropriate good practice, unless the policy gave rise or contributed to a systemic service failure.
- Complaints that concern the level of rent or service charge or the amount of the rent or service charge increase.
- Complaints that concern matters that are, or have been, the subject of legal proceedings and where a complainant has or had the opportunity to raise the subject matter of the complaint as part of those proceedings.

- Complaints that concern the terms and operation of commercial or contractual relationships not connected with the complainant's application for, or occupation of, a property for residential purposes.

- Complaints that concern terms of employment or other personnel issues, or the ending of a service tenancy following the ending of a contract of employment.

- Complaints concerning matters raised by a complainant on behalf of another without their authority.

- Complaints that fall properly within the jurisdiction of another regulator or complaints-handling body.

- Complaints that being pursued in an unreasonable manner including frivolous or vexatious complaints.

- Complaints about matters which relate to the processes and decisions concerning a member's governance structures.

8.3: The role of the designated person

This was a role introduced by the S180 of the Localism Act (2011). The effect is to introduce a further stage for a complainant to go through before being able to complain to the Housing Ombudsman. Effectively this is a filter for complaints.

When a landlord's internal complaints procedure is finished, the complainant can ask for his complaint to be considered by a 'designated person.'

That designated person may be:

- A member of the House of Commons.

- A member of the local housing authority for the district in which the property concerned is located.

- A designated tenant panel – this means a group of tenants, who are recognised by a social landlord for the purpose of referring complaints against that landlord. The Housing Ombudsman publishes a list of such panels.

A designated person will help resolve the complaint in one of two ways; they can try and resolve the complaint themselves or they can refer the complaint straight to the Ombudsman. If they refuse to do either, then the tenant complainant can contact the Ombudsman directly. Alternatively, the tenant complainant can wait 8 weeks, having exhausted the initial complaints procedure, and then go to the Ombudsman directly.

8.4: Complaints about neighbour nuisance and antisocial behaviour

If nuisance neighbours are social housing tenants and the landlord is a housing association, then a complaint should be submitted to that association, in which case the Housing Ombudsman's Scheme will apply.

8.5: The Housing Ombudsman

The Ombudsman publishes a document entitled 'The Scheme' on its website, which explains how that scheme works: http://www.housing-ombudsman.org.uk/.

As with other Ombudsman's schemes, a complainant must have exhausted the social landlord's complaints procedure before they approach the Ombudsman. The Ombudsman will not deal with the following complaints:

- Complaints that are made prior to a complainant having exhausted a member's complaints procedure.

- Complaints that are made within eight weeks of having exhausted a social landlord's complaints procedure, unless a designated person has refused to refer the complaint to the Ombudsman or has agreed to the complaint being brought to the Ombudsman, and the refusal or agreement is in writing.

- Complaints that concern the operation, process or decisions relating to the designated person's referral system

- Complaints that were brought to the Ombudsman's attention normally more than six months after they exhausted the member's complaints procedure

- Complaints that concern matters where the Ombudsman considers it quicker, fairer, more reasonable, or more effective to seek a remedy through the courts, a designated person, other tribunal, or some other procedure.

- Complaints that fall properly within the role of another Ombudsman, regulator, or complaints-handling body.

- Complaints that seek to raise matters which have already been handled.

- Complaints that concern matters which, in the Ombudsman's opinion, do not cause significant adverse effect to the complainant.

- Complaints where the complainant is seeking an outcome, which is not within the Ombudsman's authority to provide.

Members are expected to comply with the determination of the Ombudsman and they may be required to report to the Ombudsman on compliance with a determination in such a way and at such a time as the Ombudsman specifies. The Ombudsman will report a member to any appropriate regulatory agency and/or the board, committee or scrutiny panel of the member, if it fails to comply with their determination.

8.6: The Homes and Communities Agency

Social landlords are regulated by the Regulator of Social Housing, which is part of the Homes and Communities Agency, a government organisation set up by the Housing and Regeneration Act (2008). Social landlords have to comply with certain minimum standards. For instance, the 'tenancy standard' states that they are required to let their homes in a fair, transparent and efficient way and take account of the housing needs and aspirations of tenants and potential tenants.

Under S237 of the 2008 act, the regulator can actually award compensation to a person, if there has been a breach of this standard.

There is a potential overlap between what the regulator and the Ombudsman do and so the government has published a 'memorandum of understanding' between the two bodies. The memorandum says that the regulator does not monitor social landlords' performance. It only uses regulatory and enforcement powers where it judges that there has been a breach of a standard, which has or could cause serious detriment to a tenant.

However, the two bodies do work together and they meet regularly. That means that from time to time they may signpost queries or complaints to the other organisation, where appropriate, making sure to explain to the enquirer why the other organisation is the appropriate one. In practical terms, this means that the Ombudsman can report regulatory breaches to the regulator.

The Housing Ombudsman can also work with other Ombudsmen – for instance, the Local Government and Social Care Ombudsman – where the complaint falls in both of their jurisdictions.

8.7: The Draft Public Service Ombudsman Bill

This act, when it is brought into force, will abolish the Local Government and Social Care Ombudsman and the Parliamentary and Health Service Ombudsman and bring them into one office, that of the Public Service Ombudsman (PSO).

Having completed the landlord's complaints procedure, Ms F brought the complaint to the Ombudsman.

The Ombudsman encouraged the landlord to review what had gone wrong. Subsequently the landlord apologised to Ms F and her daughter and offered Ms F £750 compensation in recognition of the distress and inconvenience caused.

Housing application

http://www.housing-ombudsman.org.uk/learning-faqs/case-studies/case-study-12-housing-application-to-a-co-operative/

Ms R complained that her housing application to a housing co-operative was not dealt with appropriately. She was offered a flat but later, after she had raised concerns about the condition of the property, the offer was withdrawn.

Ms R complained to the landlord, who said that they would consider the matter at their next monthly committee meeting. However the landlord did not respond until ten months later. It raised a number of issues and suggested she had tried to sidestep the allocations process.

The Housing Ombudsman found that the landlord had not dealt appropriately with the housing application or Ms R's complaint. Furthermore, although it made a number of allegations about her, it did not provide any evidence to support these or give her the opportunity to challenge its comments. The Housing Ombudsman ordered the landlord to apologise to Ms R, pay compensation of £100, and either withdraw its allegations or provide supporting evidence.

Repairs of electrical faults

http://www.housing-ombudsman.org.uk/learning-faqs/case-studies/case-study-20-repairs-and-complaint-handling/

Ms A complained about the time taken to repair electrical faults. Following upgrade work to a number of flats in Ms A's block her electrical cooker no longer worked – she had further electrical problems over the next seven months. Ms A reported the problems to her landlord who signposted her to the private contractor who had undertaken the initial work and told her the case was closed. Ms A took her complaint to the Housing Ombudsman.

The Housing Ombudsman intervened and told the landlord it was still responsible. The landlord accepted its responsibilities, apologised and offered Ms A £600 compensation, which took into account call-out charges, time she had taken off work and mishandling of the complaint.

Pest infestation

http://www.housing-ombudsman.org.uk/learning-faqs/case-studies/case-study-30-pest-infestation-and-complaint-handling-formally-resolved/

Mr M reported pest infestation (ants) to his landlord. A local authority inspection of the block found that there was an infestation in a number of flats and that this was affecting residents' health. The local authority said it would serve a notice on the landlord to deal with the infestation but would give the landlord a chance to deal with it independently first. The landlord did not do so until after it had been served a notice.

The Housing Ombudsman investigated and concluded there had been maladministration. It ordered the landlord to pay Mr M £500 compensation for not investigating and treating the infestation promptly and a further £100 for the delays in handling the complaint. The Housing Ombudsman also recommended it review and update its pest policy.

Repairs of a leak – severe maladministration

http://www.housing-ombudsman.org.uk/learning-faqs/case-studies/case-study-43-repairs-and-complaints-handling-formally-resolved-maladministration-and-severe-maladministration/

Mr N complained to his landlord about a leak in his bedroom wall. The landlord did not follow its own published policy in dealing with Mr N's complaints nor did it respond to regular contact from the Housing Ombudsman until the Housing Ombudsman advised the landlord that it would be carrying out an investigation. The landlord took 22 months to repair the leak.

The Housing Ombudsman ordered the landlord to pay £1100 for the inconvenience of the poor repairs service and a further £400 for the distress and inconvenience of the complaint.

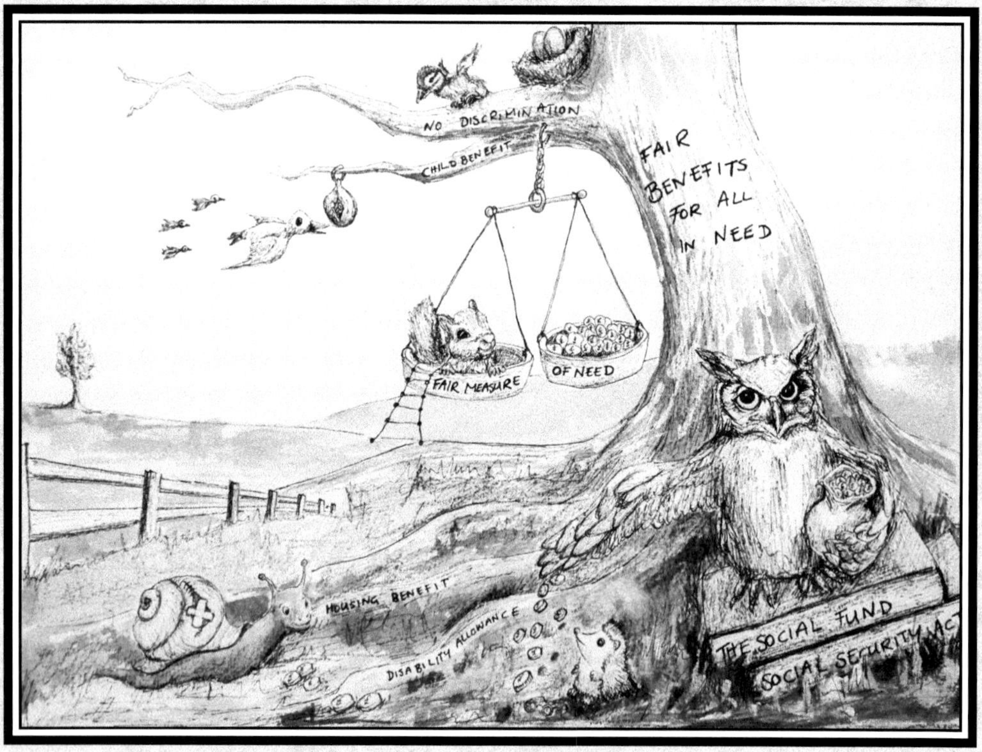
NO DISCRIMINATION
CHILD BENEFIT
FAIR BENEFITS FOR ALL IN NEED
FAIR MEASURE
OF NEED
HOUSING BENEFIT
DISABILITY ALLOWANCE
THE SOCIAL FUND
SOCIAL SECURITY ACT

Chapter 9: Complaints about benefits

9.1: Introduction

The Department for Work and Pensions (DWP) publishes its complaints procedure at: https://www.gov.uk/government/organisations/department-for-work-pensions/about/complaints-procedure.

This simple procedure covers most types of benefits including state pensions. It does not cover child maintenance, which is administered by the Child Maintenance Service and overseen by the Parliamentary and Health Services Ombudsman.

There are also two types of benefits (housing and council tax benefit) which are paid/administered by local authorities. This means that any complaints about those benefits come under the local authority's complaints system and, ultimately, the Local Government and Social Care Ombudsman.

9.2: Complaints and the appeals system for benefits

When a client is unhappy about a benefits decision, it is very important to distinguish between the complaints procedure and the appeals system. The appeals system is beyond the scope of this book but it is explained on the DWP website linked above; it has particular time limits and can end up before a tribunal or even a court. The complaints procedure is intended to deal with:

- mistakes that have been made in the payment of benefits
- unreasonable delays
- how a benefits applicant has been treated
- not being kept informed.

9.3: How to submit a complaint – the procedure

The complaint can be submitted in writing or by telephone, or in person. There is an online complaints system for jobseekers allowance and universal credit.

The procedure set out by the DWP does not appear to set out a time limit for making a complaint, other than saying that it should be made as soon as possible.

If the complainant is not satisfied with the initial response, or there needs to be a further investigation, then the complainant can ask for the complaint to go to a 'complaint resolution manager', who will contact the complainant, usually by telephone to talk about the complaint and agree on how to investigate it. They will contact the complainant again within 15 working days to tell them the outcome or to explain when the complainant can expect a response, if it is going to take longer.

If the complaint resolution manager cannot resolve the complaint, then the complainant will be asked whether they want the complaint to go to a senior manager. If the complainant agrees, the senior manager will ask for an independent internal review of the complaint and will contact the complainant within 15 working days to tell them the outcome or when they can expect a response, if it is going to take longer.

The complainant then has the option of asking the independent case examiner (ICE) to look at the complaint. The complainant must contact the ICE within six months of getting the final response from the DWP. The complainant must also send the ICE a copy of that final response.

9.4: The role of the Parliamentary and Health Service Ombudsman

If that complainant is not satisfied with the response form the ICE, they can then ask their MP (or any other MP) to send their complaint to the Parliamentary and Health Service Ombudsman.

Schedule 3 to the Parliamentary Commissioners Act 1967 excludes various matters from the remit of the PHSO. This include other legal avenues, such as litigation against a government department and it would include a matter that can be pursued through a benefits tribunal.

There is also a time limit for applying to the PHSO, which is generally twelve months from the date 'on which the person aggrieved first had notice of the matters alleged in the complaint'.

See Chapter 6 for more information about the PHSO and their website: www.ombudsman.org.uk.

9.5: Key points

- The DWP complaints procedure covers most types of benefits but not all – housing and council tax benefits are covered by the local authority's complaints system and child maintenance by the Child Maintenance Service.

- It is very important to distinguish between the complaints procedure and the appeals system for benefits decisions.

- The complaints procedure is intended to deal with: mistakes with the payment of benefits, unreasonable delays, treatment of an applicant, and not being kept informed.

- The complaint can be submitted in writing or by telephone, or in person. It should be made as soon as possible.

- The next stage up from the initial complaint is to go to a complaint resolution manager, and after that a senior manager.

- The complainant then has the option of asking the independent case examiner (ICE) to look at the complaint.

- The complaints system is subject to the Parliamentary and Health Service Ombudsman.

INNOCENT UNTIL PROVEN GUILTY
CONFIDENTIALITY
INTEGRITY
HONESTY
JUSTICE
CORRUPTION WILL NOT
BE TOLERATED
NO BULLYING
POLICE
HUMAN RIGHTS
BALANCING SECURITY
& CIVIL LIBERTIES

Chapter 10: Complaints about the police and the crown prosecution service

10.1: Introduction

This chapter concerns the rights of people, whether they are adults or children, to make complaints to the police. The police force is a public institution, which is given various powers (such as the right to arrest) so that it can protect and serve the community. As with other public institutions, such as local authorities, the police have to exercise their powers in the right way and they have to secure and maintain public confidence in the system. They cannot abuse those powers or discriminate against people. If they do, then not only will they be subject to a complaint but they may also be subject to a claim for compensation by the complainant. Compensation claims against the police require the advice of a specialist solicitor.

Police forces are divided up into areas of the country, for instance the Metropolitan Police covers the Greater London area. Each police force is headed by a chief constable (although in London it is a commissioner). That chief constable or 'chief officer' is responsible for the overall running and performance of the force.

Local policing bodies (for most areas of the country, police and crime commissioners) are responsible for making sure the chief officer is delivering proper policing services in their area. They should also ensure that the chief officer has appropriate processes in place for dealing with complaints.

The Police Reform Act (2002) set up a new complaint system for the police. The Police Reform and Social Responsibility Act (2011) amended the complaints system; it was designed to streamline the process, ensure that complaints are handled at the lowest appropriate level, and focus more on putting things right for members of the public.

Further changes were made to the complaints system by the Policing and Crime Act (2017), which changed the name of the body that deals with complaints against the police from the Independent Police Complaints Commission to the Independent Office for Police Conduct (IOPC). The act also reforms the complaints system, including the way in which the IOPC is run. It also provides for a new system of 'super complaints' to be made by certain designated bodies and confers new protections on police whistle blowers.

10.2: The Independent Office for Police Conduct (formerly the Independent Police Complaints Commission)

In January 2018, the Independent Police Complaints Commission became the Independent Office for Police Conduct (IOPC). It is different from the Ombudsman, insofar as it deals with certain more serious complaints from the outset and it works very closely with police forces, within the complaints procedure.

The IOPC is a body funded by the Home Office but it is completely independent of the government and the police. It is run by a chair and commissioners and, by law, they must not have worked for the police in any capacity prior to their appointment.

The IOPC oversees the process and sets the standards that the police should follow when they handle complaints. As with complaints against local authorities and hospitals, the majority of complaints are submitted first of all to the police force that is the subject of the complaint. That complaint is then usually handled by a supervisor or manager or a person who works in the department within the force that deals with complaints. As with other complaints systems, the police are expected to learn from their mistakes.

The IOPC's website can be found at: www.policeconduct.gov.uk. It contains clear and easy-to-understand information about how to make a complaint to the police and is a good first stop for anyone considering doing so. It also has a news archive, which contains the results of its investigations across the country.

The IOPC has published a short guide to its complaints procedure on its website at www.policeconduct.gov.uk/complaints-and-appeals/make-complaint. It provides a helpful online system for finding the relevant policing body and submitting a complaint to them.

Police forces must refer certain complaints and incidents to the IOPC – for example; an allegation that an officer has seriously assaulted someone or committed a serious sexual offence; an allegation that an officer has exploited someone for a sexual purpose; or if someone has died or been seriously injured following direct or indirect contact with the police. Typically in shooting incidents, the IOPC will be called upon to investigate immediately after the event.

10.3: The complaints system – an overview

The actual structure of the complaints system is set out in Schedule 3 of the Police Reform Act and the Police (Complaints and Misconduct) Regulations (2012). The system covers both police officers and civilian employees. Straightforward complaints are generally dealt with by a process called 'local handling' and more serious complaints will be dealt with by investigations involving the IOPC.

The police complaints system does not provide for compensation. If the police admit fault, then they may make an apology or possibly take action to change the way in which they are doing something. If the complaint is handled by the IOPC, they may make recommendations to the police. In more serious cases involving misconduct by a police officer, there may be disciplinary or even criminal proceedings against that officer. However, the system does not include the power to award financial compensation, for instance for injury or some other financial loss. That is a matter where the complaint should seek the advice of a specialist lawyer.

The IOPC publishes an easy-to-read guide on its website. However, there is also statutory guidance, which as stated above is subject to change. The Policing and Crime Act (2017) will make changes to this statutory guidance. These will take effect at different times. As changes start to take effect, parts of this statutory guidance will become out of date. We expect all of the changes to be in place by early 2019.

The statutory guidance is quite long but is probably the best guide for advocates, particularly those assisting with complex or serious complaints. We will be referring to this 'statutory guidance' in this chapter. The statutory guidance draws on good practice in complaints handling and, in particular, the Parliamentary and Health Ombudsman's 'principles of good complaints handling'. These are:

- getting it right
- being customer focused
- being open and accountable
- acting fairly and proportionately
- putting things right
- seeking continuous improvement.

The statutory guidance admits that the police complaints system is not straightforward or easy to understand, even for lawyers, and it can be very difficult for complainants. Certainly, the procedure is considerably more complex than the complaints procedures we have seen for adult and children's social care, or for hospitals and doctors. As such, it is strongly recommended that advocates try to familiarise themselves with the statutory guidance, particularly when making a complaint about a particularly serious, complex, or unusual matter.

Local police forces are expected, under the statutory guidance, to provide their own information about the complaints system on their websites. Information has to be easy to find, clear, accurate, comprehensible and up to date. The IOPC also expects the police to include a link to information about the complaints system on the front page of their websites.

10.4: Complaints concerning discrimination

The statutory guidance recognises the importance of the police service being seen to be fairly policing a diverse society. It also states that people dealing with complaints should be trained additionally in identifying discrimination and recognising that discrimination is not always overt.

Separate guidelines for discrimination complaints can be found at: https://policeconduct.gov.uk/sites/default/files/Documents/research-learning/guidelines_for_handling_allegations_of_discrimination.pdf. This guidance should be read by anyone assisting with a complaint about discrimination.

10.5: Who can make a complaint?

S12 of The Police Reform Act (2002) says that a complaint may be made by any of the following:

- A member of the public who is complaining about something done to them by the police.

- A member of the public who has been adversely affected by something the police has done.

- A member of the public who has witnessed the police doing something, about which they wish to complain.

- A person acting on behalf of a person falling within any of the above.

There is nothing to stop a child making a complaint, although in the case of a child under 16 years old, the police may need to ascertain whether that person has a suitable person or advocate to help them through the process. The statutory guidance states that written consent from the child for someone else to present the complaint will be required.

Complainants are mostly unrepresented by formal advocates. Consequently, the IOPC's website and its statutory guidance need to be studied before a complaint is submitted.

10.6: Who can be complained about?

Under this complaints system, members of the public can make complaints against local policing bodies. They can also make complaints against the:

- Home Office.
- Her Majesty's Revenue and Customs.
- Mayor's Office for Policing and Crime.
- Police and Crime Commissioners.
- Gangmasters and Labour Abuse Authority.

10.7: Time limits

The police can refuse to deal with a complaint – the term they use is that they can 'disapply' it – if more than 12 months have passed since the incident giving rise to the complaint and if there is no good reason for the delay or an injustice would be likely to be caused by the delay.

10.8: What can be complained about – conduct, 'direction and control' and death and serious injury (DSI) matters

A complaint can be made not only about the conduct of a particular police officer, but also wider issues such as strategic decisions taken by the police. For example, members of the public may complain about the decision to put more police in a particular area or the decision to (or not to) arrest and prosecute a particular suspect for a certain crime. Complaints can also be made about the conduct of police officers who are off duty if that conduct discredits the police service or undermines public confidence in it.

The complaints system distinguishes between three different types of complaints. The distinction is important because parts of the process, including the right of appeal, will be different. Complainants should try to establish what type of complaint they are making.

- Complaints about conduct.
- Complaints about 'direction and control' of the police.
- Death and serious injury matters (DSI for short).

Conduct complaints will be, quite simply, where the complainant has been aggrieved by the conduct (actions and/or behaviour) of one or more members of the policing body. Most complaints by members of the public will fall into this category as most interactions with the police are at this level.

Complaints about the direction and control of the police covers:

- Complaints about operational decisions such as: force-wide crime strategies.
- The process of creating operational policing policies: for example a key community group not being consulted in a policy that affects them.
- Organisational decisions – such as the allocation of police officers to a certain locality.
- General policing standards in the force.
- Conduct on a wider level, such as the deployment of officers for a particular investigation or a decision not to arrest a suspect for a particular crime.

The right of appeal in relation to direction and control complaints is more limited than the right of appeal for conduct complaints.

DSI matters have to be referred (by the policing body) directly to the IPCC when they are made. These will obviously include incidents such as deaths in police custody or shootings by the police. They will also include incidents where someone has received a serious injury. Under Section 12 of the Police Reform Act, 'serious injury' means a fracture, a deep cut, a deep laceration or an injury causing damage to an internal organ or the impairment of any bodily function.

10.9: The initial procedure

Whenever a complaint is received, the complainant should be advised on who is dealing with the complaint and given their contact details. The statutory guidance suggests that the complainant should be contacted as soon as possible to establish exactly what the complainant is complaining about and what they would like to happen. The complainant should be contacted within two working days but this may need to be a lot sooner depending on the seriousness of the complaint. The statutory guidance emphasises that a 'personal approach' should be applied; meaning that complaint handlers should seek to engage the complainant in resolving their complaint rather than taking decisions on their own and just sending letters.

10.9.1: Recording

The first thing the police do is consider the complaint and make a decision about whether to record it. This is important because the police do not have to record certain types of complaints. The police do not have to record:

- complaints where criminal or disciplinary proceedings are being, or already have been, carried out against the person complained about
- complaints where the name and address of the complainant is not given and it is not practical to find out what these are
- complaints which are 'vexatious, oppressive or otherwise an abuse of the procedures for dealing with complaints'
- complaints which are repetitious
- complaints which are fanciful.

10.9.2: Disapplication

Even once the complaint is recorded, the police can still 'disapply' it using some of the grounds above as well as others including the 12 month time limit. It's important to note that, under certain limited circumstances, a complaint can be disapplied in the middle of an investigation. However the complainant may have the right to appeal this decision.

The investigating officer should keep an audit trail throughout the investigation. They will need to show, amongst other things, that they have taken steps to seek the views of the complainant. If the complainant wishes to submit a statement, they should be allowed to do so.

The policing body has a duty to keep the complainant informed of its progress. The first update should be within 28 days of the start of the investigation and subsequent updates should be at least every 28 days thereafter.

Once the investigation is complete, the policing body should tell the complainant by letter if the investigation has found in their favour and what action is being taken. There should also be an investigation report – this is an important document which should be clear, unambiguous and evidence-based. We will come back to the investigation report later. As with local resolution, the complainant must also be informed in writing of their right of appeal.

10.9.7: Supervised, managed and independent investigations

Once a referral is made to the IOPC (as we saw in 10.9.3) it must then determine whether the matter should be investigated. If it decides that the matter should be investigated then it must determine the mode of investigation, having regard to the seriousness of the case and the public interest.

If the IOPC decides that the matter does not need to be investigated, then it may refer the complaint back to the original policing body so that the local body may consider whether to pursue local resolution, local investigation or disapplication.

If the IOPC decides that the matter needs investigating then it must decide the mode of investigation. This could be, as we have seen, local investigation. It could also be a supervised investigation – whereby the IOPC supervises the local policing body's investigation. It could be a managed investigation – whereby the IOPC manages the local policing body's investigation. Or it could be an independent investigation – whereby the IOPC carries out the investigation itself with the cooperation of the local policing body.

The IOPC can, at any time, re-determine the mode of investigation.

10.9.8: The investigation report

In a local investigation, this is written by the investigator. In a supervised investigation the IOPC has to confirm that the terms of reference have been adhered to and the police force should confirm that the IOPC is so satisfied. In a managed investigation the investigator writes the report but should consult the IOPC's managing investigator about its findings. Sometimes the managing investigator may add an addendum to the report.

All reports should be objective and evidence-based and they should:

- explain what the complaint, conduct or DSI matter is about
- include the terms of reference, if any, for the investigation
- give a clear account of the evidence gathered
- show that the investigation has met the objectives set for it in the terms of reference or otherwise
- provide clearly reasoned conclusions based on the evidence
- highlight any learning opportunities for either an individual or the organisation, where appropriate, even where no allegation is substantiated
- be written in plain language free of technical jargon.

The investigation report will go to the policing body and, depending on the mode of investigation, to the IOPC. The policing body itself will then make its own determinations on the report and report back to the complainant. In most cases the complainant should receive a copy of the complaint themselves as the police are under a general duty to provide information. However there are certain exceptions to this duty that apply particularly when making complaints against the police. We shall turn to these now.

10.9.9: Exceptions to the duty to provide information

In the complaints systems we have already seen there is a general expectation on the body complained against to be open and transparent in its attempts to resolve the complaint and to provide information to the complainant about the steps it has taken to satisfy the complainant. However this duty to keep the complainant and interested persons informed does not apply in circumstances where the following considerations apply:

- The interests of national security.
- The prevention or detection of crime, or the apprehension or prosecution of offenders.

- Proportionality grounds (this is too complex to explain in detail here but an example could be that the cost of the investigation on the public purse would outweigh the greater good).

- The public interest.

In theory any public body could be prevented from sharing information because of these considerations however in practice it is most likely that complainants will only encounter this with complaints against the police.

The decision about whether to withhold information because of any of the above considerations lies with the police. They must balance the complainant's right for information against the other considerations, exercise their discretion, and make a judgement.

10.10: Discontinuance and suspending of a procedure

Under certain limited grounds an investigation may be stopped or 'discontinued'. When a policing body is planning to discontinue a complaint it should contact the complainant at their last known address, offering the complainant 28 days to make any representations before the policing body makes its final decision. A policing body may consider discontinuing an investigation if:

- the complainant refuses to cooperate to the extent that it is not reasonably practicable to carry out the investigation

- where it decides that the complaint is suitable for local resolution

- the complaint or matter is vexatious, oppressive or otherwise an abuse of procedures for dealing with complaints

- the complaint is repetitious

- it is not reasonably practicable to carry on with the investigation.

If the complaint is one that required referral to the IOPC, then the policing body must seek permission from the IOPC before discontinuing the investigation. They must follow the IOPC's directions.

The complainant generally has a right to appeal against a decision to discontinue an investigation.

The policing body may also suspend an investigation if it decides that to continue it would prejudice any criminal investigation or proceedings. This is a matter of judgement and discretion and the police have to carry out a balancing exercise but should consider things such as:

- Whether delay would lead to the frustration of any potential criminal or disciplinary proceedings against a person serving with the police.

- In particular, whether suspending the investigation would risk the expiration of the six-month statutory time limit for bringing a prosecution against certain offences.

- Whether delay would otherwise lead to injustice to the complainant, interested person, or to the subject of the complaint.

When the criminal proceedings/investigation has been completed the police should contact the complainant to see if they want to resume their complaint and the complaint must be resumed if the complainant so wishes.

10.11: The right of appeal

If a complainant is dissatisfied with the decision from the police, then they have the right to appeal or in other words, apply for a review of that decision. The appeal is either made to the policing body against whom the complaint was originally brought or to the IOPC. It is important that complainants are aware that appeals, under this complaints system, should involve a 'fresh consideration' not just a 'quality check' of the original decision.

An appeal must be in writing and must be in time. Appeals should state:

- the details of the complaint
- the date on which the complaint was made
- the name of the force or local policing body whose decision is the subject of the appeal
- the grounds for the appeal
- the date on which the decision, which is being appealed against, was given to the complainant.

The appeals section ('How to appeal') of the IOPC website sets out the circumstances in which an appeal is made to either body. Section 13 of the IOPC statutory guidance has a very helpful diagram, which explains this further.

There is a test, which is set out in the 2012 regulations and the statutory guidance, to determine whether that appeal should be dealt with by the IOPC or by the relevant chief officer of the policing body complained against. If a complaint satisfies any of the criteria laid down in the test, then the relevant appeal body is the IOPC. If not, the relevant appeal body is the chief officer. If the appeal is to be made to the police force, then their website will have an online procedure for that appeal to be made.

As a very general rule, appeals that are about very serious issues or that are about senior officers will be dealt with by the IOPC. If the appeal is to be made to the IOPC, then they provide an appeal form on their website. This has to be submitted and received by the IOPC within 28 days of the date on the police letter.

10.12: Complaints about the Crown Prosecution Service

The Crown Prosecution Service (CPS) is responsible for prosecuting criminal cases investigated by the police in England and Wales. They operate from various regional offices up and down the country. They are headed by the Director of Public Prosecutions and their website can be found at: www.cps.gov.uk/.

The CPS publishes *The Code for Crown Prosecutors* which sets out the circumstances in they can prosecute a crime. In brief, there are two main tests:

- Is there enough evidence against the defendant?
- Is it in the public interest for the CPS to bring the case to court?

10.13: The Code of Practice for Victims of Crime

The CPS and other agencies within the criminal justice system (such as the police) have to conduct themselves in a certain way towards victims of crime.

Some charities provide advocates for victims of crime, including Independent Domestic Violence Advocates and Independent Sexual Violence Advocates.

The Code of Practice for Victims of Crime can be found on the CPS website and it is issued under S32 of the Domestic Violence, Crime and Victims Act (2004). It is long and detailed, and it has separate chapters for adults, and for children and young persons. It is a 'must read' for anyone supporting a person going through the criminal justice system. If there is a breach of the code, then that can form the basis of a complaint against the CPS or the police.

The code covers a large number of 'service providers' within the criminal justice system including the CPS. These service providers are listed in the introduction to the code. So, for instance, the Parole Board and the National Probation Service are required to provide services in accordance with certain parts of the code.

The idea behind the code is to put victims first, make the system more responsive and easier to navigate. Victims of crime should be treated in a respectful, sensitive, tailored, and professional manner without discrimination of any kind. They should receive appropriate support to help them, as far as possible, to cope and recover and be protected from re-victimisation. It is also important that victims of crime know what information and support is available to them and from whom they can request help.

There is a list of key entitlements for victims of crime, which must be met by the various bodies covered by the code. Some of these entitlements are as follows:

- A written acknowledgement that a person has reported a crime, including the basic details of the offence.
- An enhanced service if a person is a victim of serious crime, a persistently targeted victim or a vulnerable or intimidated victim.
- A needs assessment to help work out what support a victim needs.
- Information on what to expect from the criminal justice system.
- Referral to organisations supporting victims of crime.
- Being informed about the police investigation, such as if a suspect is arrested and charged and any bail conditions imposed.
- Making a Victim Personal Statement (VPS) to explain the effect of the crime.
- Being able to read the VPS aloud or have it read aloud, subject to the views of the court, if a defendant is found guilty.
- Being informed if the suspect is to be prosecuted or not or given an out of court disposal.
- The right to seek a review of the police or CPS's decision not to prosecute in accordance with the National Police Chiefs Council (NPCC) and CPS Victims' Right to Review schemes.

The code also provides a handy route map through the criminal justice system.

10.14: The CPS complaints procedure

The CPS complaints procedure can be found on the 'Feedback and Complaints' section of their website. It is contained within a document entitled Feedback and Complaints Guidance.

It is important to distinguish between making a complaint about the way in which the CPS have acted in dealing with a victim of crime, and the right of that victim (under the Victims' Right to Review Scheme) to review a decision made by the CPS not to prosecute. We deal with that scheme below. Any member of the public who has had direct contact with the CPS can make a complaint. That complaint can be made directly by the individual concerned or on their behalf by a nominated representative such as a family member or friend, support group, solicitor, or other professional.

Complaints will only be considered if they are received within six months of the matter complained of. This appears to be a strict time limit, with no discretion to allow a complainant more time.

The complaints procedure is made up of various stages and it distinguishes between 'legal' and 'service' complaints. A legal complaint is (for instance) the decision of the CPS to prosecute someone for a particular crime, whereas a service complaint is about the way in which the CPS has behaved towards a complainant. The guidance gives examples.

It is possible to have a complaint resolved by 'early resolution' prior to the formal process, which works in three stages.

Stage 1 involves the relevant manager of the CPS office. The complainant can then go to Stage 2, where the complaint is handled by the relevant deputy/chief crown prosecutor or deputy/casework division head. This will be the end of the process for complaints relating to legal decisions (for instance decisions not to prosecute) made by the CPS.

Stage 3 is a referral of the complaint to the Independent Assessor of Complaints (IAC) for review. The IAC operates independently from the CPS and is responsible for handling and investigating complaints from members of the public in relation to the quality of the service provided by the CPS and its adherence to its published complaints procedure.

Victims then have the opportunity to refer their complaint to the Parliamentary and Health Service Ombudsman via an MP, following the IAC's review. For more information about the PHSO, see Chapter 6 and their website: www.ombudsman.org.uk.

The Draft Public Service Ombudsman Bill will transfer the PHSO into the new office of the Public Service Ombudsman.

10.15: The Witness Charter

The government has also published a charter for witnesses, which sets out the standards of care for witnesses in the criminal justice system. In particular this sets out special measures for vulnerable and intimidated witnesses, including (for instance) the appointment of a registered intermediary for people with learning difficulties. It also set out the kind of support that witnesses can expect through the prosecution process, including safety at court. The charter can be found at: www.gov.uk/government/publications/the-witness-charter-standards-of-care-for-witnesses-in-the-criminal-justice-system.

10.16: The Victims' Right to Review Scheme

The Crown Prosecution Service and other service providers are required to provide victims with a right to review a decision not to prosecute. The service provider must provide such a right at least in respect of serious offences (as determined by the service provider) and they will set out their own rules for asking for a review.

The CPS has a 'Victims' Right to Review Scheme', which can be found on their website. This explains the procedure. Very briefly the victim can contact the CPS office where the decision not to prosecute was made. The time limit is very tight. The CPS encourages victims to make their request for a review within five working days. They also say that they will consider requests for review for up to three months from the communication of the decision not to prosecute.

10.17: The Child Sexual Abuse Review Panel

Where a child under the age of 18 years old alleges that they were the victim of a sexual offence, but the police or the CPS decided that no action should be taken at the time, that person can ask the panel to look at the case again, if they are not satisfied that the original allegations were dealt with appropriately.

The panel considers whether the approach taken in any case where the police or CPS previously advised against taking further action was wrong, and advises whether the allegations should be reinvestigated by the police or the prosecution decision reviewed by the CPS. The case will be referred back to the police force (or CPS area) from where the case originated for them to decide on the action to be taken. Further details about the panel can be found on the CPS website.

10.18: The Victims' Commissioner

This office was set up by S48 of the Domestic Violence, Crime and Victims Act (2004). It does not deal with individual complaints but rather its role is to promote the interests of victims and witnesses; encourage good practice in the treatment of victims and witnesses; and keep under review the operation of the Code of Practice for Victims of Crime. Its website has useful information about making a complaint and it can be found at: https://victimscommissioner.org.uk/vc-standards.

10.19: Key points

- The police are a public institution, which has to exercise its powers in the right way and it has to secure and maintain public confidence in the system.

- The system has been changed as from January 2018 with the implementation of the Policing and Crime Act (2017), but those changes will happen gradually. Consequently advocates need to check the updated guidance on the IOPC's website.

- The IOPC's statutory guidance is the best guide for advocates.

- The police can refuse to deal with a complaint or 'disapply' it, if more than 12 months have elapsed.

- The police complaints procedure varies according to the type of complaint made. If a complainant is dissatisfied with the decision from the police, then they have the right to appeal. The appeal is either made to the police force against whom the complaint is made or the IOPC.

- The Crown Prosecution Service (CPS) is responsible for prosecuting criminal cases investigated by the police. They (and other law enforcement agencies) have to operate within the Code of Practice for Victims of Crime.

- The CPS complaints procedure can be found on the 'Feedback and Complaints' section of their website.

- Complaints will only be considered if they are received within six months.
- At the end of the complaints procedure, victims have the opportunity to refer their complaint to the Parliamentary and Health Service Ombudsman (PHSO), via an MP, following the Independent Assessor of Complaint's review.
- The government has also published a Witness Charter, which sets out the standards of care for witnesses in the criminal justice system.
- The Crown Prosecution Service and other service providers are required to provide victims with a right to review a decision not to prosecute. They do this through a Victims Right to Review Scheme.
- The Child Sexual Abuse Review Panel will also look at decisions not to prosecute in certain cases involving sex offences against children.
- The Victims' Commissioner promotes the interests of victims and witnesses.

GLOBAL ENERGY
UTILITIES COMPANY
FAIR ACCESS TO THE
EARTH'S RESOURCES

Chapter 11: Complaints about utility and other private companies

11.1: Introduction

As we saw in Chapter 3, the concept of the Ombudsman covers both the public and the private sector. Whilst the Local Government and Social Care Ombudsman and the Parliamentary and Health Services Ombudsman are funded by the government, other Ombudsmen are funded by their members, who agree to operate complaints procedures that are subject to those Ombudsmen.

11.2: Utility services

Providers of utility services are heavily regulated by the government. Gas and electricity is regulated by the Office of Gas and Electricity Markets (Ofgem), water by the Water Services Regulation Authority (Ofwat) and postal services and telecommunications by the Office of Communications (Ofcom).

The utility regulators do not normally deal with individual complaints about a service but they do monitor what utility companies do and might well take action against a utility provider if they were consistently failing to operate a proper complaints procedure. Their websites provide information about complaints procedures and the kind of complaint that may be referred to them.

S42 to S52 of the Consumers, Estate Agents and Redress Act (2007) require gas, electricity and water providers to have complaints procedures in place and conform to certain standards.

The regulations that flow from this 2007 act are written with vulnerable people in mind. For instance, Regulation 8 of the Gas and Electricity (Consumer Complaints Handling Standards) Regulations (2008) requires regulated providers to establish arrangements to deal with the investigation of vulnerable consumer complaints and the investigation of complaints relating to disconnection of gas or electricity. Regulated providers should also take necessary or appropriate additional steps to resolve consumer complaints that involve vulnerable consumers. These regulations also set out detailed provisions as to how gas and electricity providers should operate their complaints procedures.

S38 and S39 of the Water Industry Act (1991) provides powers to the government to make regulations setting out customer service standards that must be met by water providers. S95 and S96 make similar provisions in relation to sewerage providers.

As with the gas and electricity regulations, those regulations that flow from the Water Industry Act are written with the particular hazards of water and sewerage supply in mind. For instance, Regulation 11 of the Water Supply and Sewerage Services (Customer Service Standards) Regulations (2008) provides for compensation to be paid in relation to flooding from sewers.

S51 of the Postal Services Act (2011) allows the regulator, Ofcom, to impose consumer protection conditions on providers of postal services. These conditions include the requirement to have redress schemes in place.

S27E of the Telecommunications Act (1984) requires providers to establish complaints procedures for their customers.

Citizens Advice (the operating name of the National Association of Citizens Advice Bureaux) operates a free consumer service that helps people with utility problems. Their website can be found at: www.citizensadvice.org.uk and it contains easy to read information about dealing with utility problems.

11.3: Procedures for complaining to utility companies

Utility companies are required to publish their procedures on their website and provide details of sources of help.

The procedures for making a complaint to a utility company are generally simpler than those that we have seen in previous chapters. The complaint is brought direct to the utility company, which may prescribe one or more stages in order to try and resolve the complaint.

11.4: Utility Ombudsmen and the water industry redress scheme

Ombudsman Services is a national private sector Ombudsman scheme, which independently resolves complaints between consumers and companies that are signed-up members. Each member pays a subscription as well as case fees to consider each complaint. Their website can be found at: www.ombudsman-services.org.

Ombudsman Services cover both the communications and energy sectors. Major communications and energy utility companies such as British Gas and British Telecom are members of Ombudsman Services and each sector publishes a list of companies that are signed up to its scheme.

Water and sewerage services are not included within the remit of Ombudsman Services. Complaints that have gone through a water company's procedure can then go to the Consumer Council for Water: www.ccwater.org.uk. Thereafter the complaint may be eligible to go to the Water Industry Redress Scheme: www.waters.org.uk.

11.5: Consumer complaints in other sectors

11.5.1: Consumer protection law

The law provides various protections for consumers. One of the main statutes is the Consumer Rights Act (2015). In this section, when we refer to a 'consumer', we mean an individual buying something (whether it be goods or services) otherwise than in the course of business. At the same time, we also refer to 'traders'. This is not just someone selling fruit in a marketplace. It is a person who is acting in the course of any trade, business, craft or profession, which would include lawyers and accountants.

Professional people tend to be heavily regulated and so they will be subject to other rules. Businesses that provide financial services are subject to a whole raft of complex legislation. We examine complaints procedures against lawyers in Chapter 14.

Consequently, consumer protection laws provide the bare minimum of what is expected from a 'trader' dealing with a 'consumer'.

11.5.2: Complaints procedures for consumers

As with utility companies, complainants are expected to go through the company's internal complaints procedure before they are allowed to refer their complaint up to an Ombudsman.

Some of these Ombudsmen do not use the title, Ombudsman. They are referred to as Alternative Dispute Resolution (ADR) providers or Dispute Resolution bodies. So for instance, the Association of Chartered Certified Accountants is the Dispute Resolution body for accountants. ADR and Dispute Resolution effectively describe what an Ombudsman does.

When making a complaint against any kind of private company, it is important to look at their complaints procedures and in particular to look at whether they are regulated or members of a professional/trade body.

For example, chartered surveyors are regulated by the Royal Institution of Chartered Surveyors (RICS), whilst letting agents are regulated by the Association of Residential Managing Agents (ARMA). These professional/trade bodies may require a member to have a complaints procedure in place and to operate it. It is well worth checking the website of the organisation to see what it says about complaints procedures and, in particular, whether there is an Ombudsman/ADR provider to whom a complaint can be referred. That Ombudsman/ADR provider's website may also provide further useful information such as case studies of complaints.

11.5.3: The obligation to refer consumers to Alternative Dispute Resolution (ADR)

European Community law requires that consumers have legal protection. One relatively recent European law (EU Directive 2013/11/EU) requires the UK to ensure that most disputes between a consumer and a trader can be submitted to ADR.

This European directive has been implemented into UK law by the Alternative Dispute Resolution for Consumer Disputes (Competent Authorities and Information) Regulations 2015. The Chartered Trading Standards Institute (CTSI) now operates as the competent authority auditing and approving Ombudsman/ADR bodies in all non-regulated sectors as per the requirements of the legislation. Their website can be found at: www.tradingstandards.uk.

Regulation 19 of the 2015 regulations sets out traders' obligations when dealing with complaints. The following is guidance from CTSI, which it has set out on its website.

When a consumer and trader come into dispute over goods or services bought from the trader, the law now requires that the trader supply the consumer with details of an ADR body capable of dealing with the complaint. The trader is not required to actually use the services of the ADR body but they are required to indicate to the consumer if they will do so or not. Although not generally required to use ADR many traders recognise the benefits in customer relations in doing so. Others are required to use ADR through the terms of their membership of a trade association or by operating in a sector regulated by government. Although traders are required by law to provide this information, they are not obliged to engage in the ADR process except where they operate in a sector which is mandated to do so by statute or by membership of a trade association.

11.5.4: Various consumer Ombudsmen/ADR bodies

CTSI publish on their website a list of some 40 Ombudsmen/ADR bodies: https://ec.europa.eu/consumers/odr/main/index.cfm?event=main.adr.show.

The following are examples of Ombudsmen/ADR providers in various sectors.

Ombudsman Services has a property sector which includes complaints about chartered surveyors, estate agents, residential managing or letting agents and valuers.

There is also an alternative Ombudsman for the property sector. This is the property Ombudsman whose website can be found at: https://www.tpos.co.uk. As with Ombudsman Services, they have their own membership.

The consumer sector of Ombudsman Services handles complaints about faulty goods/service, poor service, failed/incomplete or non-delivery of goods or services, shoddy workmanship and pricing issues. Ombudsman Services are an accredited ADR entity under these regulations.

The number of companies on the Consumer Ombudsman is small and it is not compulsory for companies to be a member of the scheme. However, according to Which Magazine, the Consumer Ombudsman has said it will contact the company involved to progress the complaint on behalf of the customer, even if the company is not a member.

There is a further ADR scheme for consumers provided by RetailADR whose website can be found at: www.retailadr.org.uk. This is run by Consumer Dispute Resolution Limited (CDRL). CDRL is accredited under the 2015 regulations (see above) and it has a list of members (including several well-known high street outlets). It also operates other ADR schemes for aviation as well as a scheme for communications and utilities complaints that are not covered by Ombudsman Services.

Financial institutions (i.e. banks and building societies) are required by law to have their own complaints procedures. They are subject to the Financial Ombudsman, whose website can be found at: www.financial-ombudsman.org.uk.

Vehicle sales and servicing have the Motor Ombudsman, which is a member of the Ombudsman Association and which has a list of accredited members. Its website can be found at: www.themotorombudsman.org.uk.

11.6: Key points

- Providers of utility services such as gas, electricity, water and communications are regulated by the government.

- These utility companies are required by law to have complaints procedures in place.

- Energy and communications companies have their own Ombudsmen. Water companies have the Water Industry Redress Scheme.

- The law also provides statutory protection for consumers in other kinds of sectors and, in particular, the obligation to refer a consumer to Alternative Dispute Resolution (ADR) where there is a dispute.

- Complainants should look at a trader's complaints procedure and whether they are a member of an association that requires them to have such a procedure.

- The Chartered Trading Standards Institute publishes on their website a list of some 40 Ombudsmen/ADR bodies.

SENSITIVE
DATA
DATA PROTECTION ACT 1998
YOUR PERSONAL
DATA MUST BE
KEPT SECURE

Chapter 12: Complaints about data protection

12.1: Introduction

The right to see a person's records is a serious issue for advocates and their clients. The consequences of a person's records or their own sensitive information falling into the wrong hands can be devastating. The legal consequences of non-compliance with data protection law are also very serious. In April 2017, the Information Commissioner fined 11 charities for breaking the law when handling donors' personal information. These fines can be very large indeed.

In this chapter, we look very briefly at how the law protects information and offer advice on what advocates can do about it.

12.2: The Information Commissioner

The Data Protection Act (1998) sets up the office of the Information Commissioner, who oversees data protection in this country. The website is: www.ico.org.uk.

This website contains a great deal of helpful information for the general public on data protection. For instance, it has a template letter for making a 'Subject Access Request' and detailed guidance on making a request (which we will come back to later in this chapter).

The Data Protection Act requires every organisation that processes personal information to register with the Information Commissioner's Office, unless they are exempt. Failure to do so is a criminal offence. Those organisations are also required to comply with the act. There are more than 400,000 registered organisations and the Information Commissioner has a list of each of them and the kind of processing that they do.

There is no complaints system for data protection equivalent to the ones that exist for adult and social care. There is no data protection Ombudsman.

However, the Information Commissioner's website allows a person to report a 'concern' about 'accessing' information: www.ico.org.uk/concerns/getting/.

12.3: The Data Protection Act (1998) – data, processing, controllers and subjects

This act is the basis of data protection legislation. It says that data is information that can be held in a paper filing system or on a computer. It calls disclosure and the use of data, 'processing'. Processing is very much wider that simply the disclosure of information. It includes:

- the organisation, adaptation or alteration of the information or data
- the retrieval, consultation or use of the information or data
- the disclosure of the information or data by transmission, dissemination or otherwise making available
- the alignment, combination, blocking, erasure or destruction of the information or data.

A 'data controller' is the person or organisation who decides how data is to be processed. A 'data processor' actually carries out the disclosure and use. A 'data subject' means an individual who is the subject of personal data, and 'personal data' means data which relate to a living individual who can be identified from that data.

So a data controller, such as a local authority, that wrongly destroys social services records on a child, could be in breach of the Data Protection Act. It will also be in breach if it refuses to disclose those records to an adult care leaver although, as we will see in this chapter, there are a number of situations where records can be legally withheld or redacted.

12.4: The data protection principles

Schedule 1 to the Data Protection Act contains eight principles, which govern the way in which the act is followed:

- **Personal data has to be processed fairly and lawfully** – this is simply another way of saying that people and organisations that hold records and process them, have to comply with the act. However, data sharing is essential for some organisations, particularly those involved in social care. For this reason, the act specifically permits certain types of disclosure if they relate to certain matters including: crime prevention and prosecution, health, education, and social work.

- **Personal data can only be obtained for one or more specified and lawful purposes, and must not be further processed in any manner incompatible with that purpose or those purposes** – if, for instance, a social worker obtained records from the police in the course of a child protection investigation simply because they were personally interested in the case, that would be a breach of the act (as well as serious misconduct on the part of the police and the social worker). There would be no breach if the information was obtained for the purposes of a child protection investigation and then that information was used for that investigation and subsequent care proceedings.

- **Personal data must be adequate, relevant and not excessive in relation to the purpose or purposes for which it is processed** – this principle encourages organisations such as local authorities to keep good records.

- **Personal data must be accurate and, where necessary, kept up to date** – it is possible for a person to get their records changed, if there is information contained in them which is inaccurate. So, for instance, a person who is shown in social services records as having a criminal record, where in fact they have no record at all, would be entitled to have that record changed. Inevitably with social services records there may be all manner of allegations about a person in the records, which constitutes available information and on which social services may rely, or which they may dismiss. It may be very much more difficult to have that information removed.

- **Personal data processed for any purpose or purposes must not be kept for longer than is necessary for that purpose or those purposes** – this principle encourages people not to hang on to data forever. The act does not actually say how long data should be retained.

However, there are rules for local authorities and others who look after children or arrange adoptions. The Care Planning, Placement and Case Review (England) Regulations (2010) require records for looked after children to be retained for 75 years from birth, or 15 years after death, whichever is earlier. Previously that duty was contained in the Arrangement for Placement of Children Regulations (1991). The same duty applies to voluntary organisations (such as private fostering agencies) under the Arrangements for Placement of Children by Voluntary Organisations and Others (England) Regulations (2011).

12.6: What can people do if their rights under the Data Protection Act are breached?

S13 of the act says that an individual who suffers damage by reason of any breach by a data controller of any of the requirements of the act is entitled to compensation.

12.6.1: Court claims

Unfortunately, this means making a claim, which will mean consulting a lawyer, and which may lead to the issue of court proceedings. These kinds of claims can also be brought under different areas of the law, such as misuse of private information and breach of confidence, which are outside the scope of this book.

Many breaches of the act are far too small for a lawyer to be able to take on but the wrongful disclosure of social services or medical information can cause a great deal of distress and even psychiatric damage. The following cases demonstrate how much the courts award in these cases.

Armoniene v Lithuania [2009] EMLR 7 – an award of €6,500 (about £5,800 at the time) was made to a person whose HIV diagnosis was made public in a newspaper.

Crook v Chief Constable of Essex Police [2015] EWHC 988 (QB) – a man was wrongly placed on a 'Most Wanted' press release by Essex Police. He recovered £5,000 for psychiatric injury, together with loss of earnings of £57,750, as well as £2,000 for distress and aggravated damages of £3,000.

There was also a recent (informal) report of a settlement of £75,000 by Greater Manchester Police to a victim of domestic abuse whose private information had been wrongly disclosed by police officers: https://informm.wordpress.com/2016/08/16/privacy-and-the-police-damages-of-75000-for-disclosure-of-private-information-nick-mcaleenan/

Gulati and Others v MGN [2015] 1482 (Ch) – this judgment is about the phone hacking cases involving a number of celebrities (including Paul Gascoigne, Sadie Frost and Alan Yentob) and the Mirror Group. It was alleged that the Mirror Group had authorised the hacking of celebrities' telephones so that embarrassing articles could published about them. Very high awards to various victims of phone hacking were made, including damages for distress ranging from £10,000 to £30,000.

12.6.2: Using the complaints system

The Information Commissioner does not have a complaints procedure. Their function under the Data Protection Act is to take enforcement proceedings against someone (i.e. a local authority) who is in breach of the act. They can levy fines (and the fines can be very substantial) but they cannot compensate a person whose data protection rights have been breached. Furthermore, they may not be prepared to act in any given case.

We set out four case reports below and overleaf; in two the local authority investigated and compensated breaches of the Data Protection Act; in the other two they referred the matter to the Information Commissioner. It appears that where the complaint is solely about data protection issues, the Local Government and Social Care Ombudsman (LGSCO) will refer the matter to the Information Commissioner. However, where data protection issues are mixed up with other types of issues, i.e. poor service, then the LGSCO may be prepared to deal with all of them together.

In cases of doubt, the writers advise making a complaint to the LGSCO and writing also to the Information Commissioner's Office (ICO), specifying the data protection breach.

Bailiffs – proper adherence to Data Protection Act principles

http://www.lgo.org.uk/information-centre/news/2015/jul/councils-urged-to-ensure-complaints-about-contractors-are-handled-properly

This was a complaint about the action of bailiffs, which resulted in the Local Government and Social Care Ombudsman recommending to the local authority that it provide evidence that the bailiff's firm had taken action to ensure all its bailiffs knew the importance of the code covering courtesy, identification, proper adherence to Data Protection Act principles, and the correct approach to seizure of third party goods.

Private care provider – destruction of care records

http://www.lgo.org.uk/information-centre/news/2014/mar/LGSCO-issues-first-adverse-findings-notice-into-surrey-private-care-provider

This was a complaint about the action of a care provider. The Local Government and Social Care Ombudsman recommended (amongst other things) that the provider apologise to the complainant for the failures identified in the findings, to review its procedures so that records were held in compliance with the Data Protection Act and to make a payment to the complainant of £250 for the uncertainty caused by the destruction of care records.

Sharing of adoption records – referred to the ICO
http://www.lgo.org.uk/decisions/children-s-care-services/adoption/16-015-467

The complainant complained that the local authority had committed a data protection breach by sharing her family's personal information with the birth father of their adoptive children. The local authority had investigated the matter. It found no evidence that it had disclosed or shared this information with the birth father. The final decision was that the Local Government and Social Care Ombudsman would not investigate this complaint and that data protection complaints were for the Information Commissioner's Office to consider.

Failure to provide adoption records – referred to the ICO
http://www.lgo.org.uk/decisions/children-s-care-services/adoption/15-017-743

The complainant complained that the council failed to provide her with her adoption records. The Local Government and Social Care Ombudsman said that they normally expected someone to refer the matter to the Information Commissioner if they had a complaint about data protection. However, the Ombudsman might decide to investigate if she thought there were good reasons. The Ombudsman investigates complaints about 'maladministration' and 'service failure'. The Ombudsman provides a free service but had to use public money carefully. She might decide not to start or continue with an investigation if she believed there is another body better placed to consider this complaint. A request for information which a body might hold about a person was a subject access request under the Data Protection Act. Parliament established the Information Commissioner's Office (ICO) to decide Data Protection Act disputes. The Ombudsman would usually consider the ICO was better placed to determine the issue at the crux of Mrs X's complaint.

12.7: The Freedom of Information Act (2000)

This act is quite separate from the Data Protection Act 1998. It provides public access to information held by public authorities. Public authorities include government departments, local authorities, the NHS, state schools and police forces.

The Freedom of Information Act (2000) does not necessarily cover every organisation that receives public money. For example, it does not cover some charities that receive grants and certain private sector organisations that perform public functions. The Information Commissioner's Office publishes information about the act on its website.

The act has potential uses for advocates. A complainant might wish to highlight a difference between what a local authority says that it does, and what it actually does in practice. For instance, a local authority may say that it aims to place a certain percentage of its looked after children with foster carers within its own area. A Freedom of Information request might highlight the fact that this target has not been met. This information could act as evidence the failure of a local authority to place a child within its own area was because of a general failure, not because of any individual decision which the local authority says was taken for the child's benefit. This information could give added strength to a complaint about that decision.

12.8: The General Data Protection Regulation

This is a regulation from the European Union, which comes into force in May 2018. It introduces a legal requirement on an organisation to report a data protection breach to the ICO within a certain time. It also provides for hefty fines for breaches of data protection law, as well as reducing the time period for an organisation, such as a local authority, to provide data in response to a request. The Information Commissioner has published a guide on their website: www.ico.org.uk/for-organisations/guide-to-the-general-data-protection-regulation-gdpr/principles/.

12.9: Key points

- Most organisations that hold information on people are required to be registered with the Information Commissioner.

- The Information Commissioner is not like an Ombudsman but it does have powers to fine people and organisations that break data protection laws, and it will look at concerns that are brought to its attention.

- Data protection law is set out mainly in the Data Protection Act and it works on a number of legal principles.

- People have the right to see their records under the Data Protection Act but that right is not absolute.

- A breach of the Data Protection Act can be the subject of a court claim, which could be worth a lot of money – but expert legal advice is required.

- A breach of the Data Protection Act can be the subject of a complaint both to the organisation breaching the act and the Information Commissioner.

- The Freedom of Information Act may be useful in giving a complaint added strength.

INNOCENT UNTIL PROVEN GUILTY
ACCESS TO JUSTICE
-FAIR TRIAL FOR ALL-
Jarndyce v Jarndyce

Chapter 13: Complaints about lawyers

13.1: Introduction

There are different types of lawyers. In this chapter we deal mainly with solicitors, but it is important to realise that other types of lawyers are covered by the same complaints procedure that applies to solicitors.

Solicitors generally work either in firms or in-house for a local authority or company. At the same time, a solicitor's firm may employ other types of lawyers, such as legal executives, barristers and paralegals. A solicitors' firm is regulated by the Law Society and the Solicitors Regulation Authority.

Barristers generally work in groups known as 'chambers', in-house for a local authority or a company, or they are sometimes employed by solicitors' firms. They are regulated by the Bar Council and the Bar Standards Board. They can take on clients direct but normally they are instructed by solicitors to give specialist advice in a case and represent clients in courts and tribunals.

Chartered legal executives are regulated by the Chartered Institute of Legal Executives. The main difference between a legal executive and a solicitor is the method by which they are trained, but they have much the same status as solicitors. There are certain areas where they have to be supervised by a solicitor.

Paralegals are people working in law firms or carrying out legal work, who are not qualified. They may be very experienced and may do the majority of the work on any given case but should always be supervised by a qualified lawyer.

Licensed conveyancers, patent and trade mark attorneys, costs lawyers and notaries do very specialist types of law and they are regulated by their own regulatory bodies but again they may work for a solicitors' firm.

All of these different types of lawyer come under the Legal Services Board, which was created by the Legal Services Act (2007). Its overriding mandate is to ensure that regulation in the legal services sector is carried out in the public interest and that the interests of consumers are placed at the heart of the system.

The Legal Services Board also oversees the organisation established to handle consumer complaints about lawyers, the Legal Ombudsman (which we will come back to later in this chapter).

Most people's experience of the law is with solicitors' firms. Any employee of a solicitors' firm dealing with a client is bound by the solicitors' code of conduct and is expected to act accordingly. Solicitors are heavily regulated and they are expected to operate effective complaints procedures as well as abide by a code of conduct laid down by their professional body, the Solicitors Regulation Authority.

13.2: Instructing a solicitor

The experience of many advocates is that it is remarkably difficult to find a solicitor to take on a case. In reality, few people can afford solicitors save for where they are dealing with routine transactions and relatively straightforward matters. The gap is plugged to some extent by legal aid, insurance policies providing for legal fees, and 'no win no fee' arrangements in litigation where the legal fees are only payable if the case is won.

Legal aid is very limited. Solicitors firms that offer legally aided services will have a contract from the Legal Aid Agency that allows them to offer those services, but the contract terms and the pay rates will be limited.

Many cases are simply too small to engage a solicitor and this is where the complaints system comes in. However, the advocate will come across cases where the services of a solicitor are essential. As with other professions, solicitors can obtain accreditations (such as expertise in child law) in certain areas by demonstrating a certain amount of expertise and experience. They will advertise these accreditations on their websites and they can be useful in selecting a solicitor.

There are a number of solicitors' associations, with their own directories. The Law Society provides a list of all of its members on its 'Find a solicitor' facility, together with their specialisms, at: www.lawsociety.org.uk. Resolution, an organisation for family lawyers, has its own membership list at: www.resolution.org.uk. The government also publishes a directory of legal aid providers at: www.gov.uk/government/publications/directory-of-legal-aid-providers. The better government site to use is: https://find-legal-advice.justice.gov.uk/ which has a search facility with a geographical and specialism fields.

A solicitors' firm is generally free to decide whether or not to accept instructions in any matter, provided it does not discriminate unlawfully. The writers advise advocates to try and build up a network of suitable solicitors with various specialisms, to whom they can pick up the telephone.

It is a criminal offence for someone to call themselves a solicitor or act as a solicitor if they are not on the Law Society's membership list (S21 Solicitors Act (1974)). It is also an offence for a person to carry on any activity which is a 'reserved legal activity' when that person is not so entitled (S14 to S17 Legal Services Act (2007)). A reserved legal activity includes appearing before a court or tribunal or conducting litigation. Consequently, it is against the law for someone to pretend to be a barrister when they are not or to use any name, title, or description, which makes it seem as though they are a barrister when they are not. S84 of the Immigration and Asylum Act (1999) states that no person may provide immigration advice or immigration services unless he is a 'qualified person'. Fraudsters will prey on the vulnerable and, from time-to-time, the authorities do prosecute people who pretend to be qualified lawyers. The Solicitors Regulation Authority also regularly puts out 'scam alerts' about the misuse of solicitors' names by fraudsters. None of this means that people cannot represent themselves in court as 'litigants in person' and have friends to help them through the process.

It is relatively easy to check a lawyer's accreditation by checking with their professional body. The Solicitors Regulation Authority has a search facility: www.sra.org.uk/faqs/contact-centre/public/04-using-a-solicitor/how-find-out-solicitor-sra-regulated.page and The Bar Standards Board's Register of Barristers can be found at: https://www.barstandardsboard.org.uk/regulatory-requirements/the-barristers'-register/.

The writers would warn advocates against taking legal advice from anyone who is not subject to proper professional regulation.

13.3: The Law Society and the Solicitors Regulation Authority (SRA)

All solicitors in England and Wales are members of the Law Society, to which they pay an annual subscription. The Law Society is authorised by the statutes below to regulate and control solicitors through its regulatory body, the SRA:

- The Solicitors Act (1974).
- The Administration of Justice Act (1985).
- The Legal Services Act (2007).

The way in which solicitors are regulated is extremely complex. They have to comply with other acts of parliament and regulations; there are solicitors and barristers who specialise in the business of regulating the legal profession. It is no exaggeration to say that the SRA expects high standards of compliance. At the same time, firms that undertake legally aided work are subject to oversight by the Legal Aid Agency and they are expected to have sound systems in place for looking after their clients and their clients' cases.

It is important to realise that even the very smallest firm of solicitors will be looking after substantial sums of money, much of which belongs to their clients. They may also be handling substantial cases, where a mistake is going to have very serious consequences for the client. All solicitors are required to have insurance in place to cover any kind of professional negligence on their part.

The Law Society publishes its periodical, the Law Society Gazette, about once a week. Towards the end of the Gazette is a description of the disciplinary proceedings taken against solicitors in England and Wales, some of which have resulted in the striking off or expulsion of individual solicitors, the closure of firms and action taken against lawyers to stop them working again in another law firm.

13.4: The Solicitors Regulation Authority's code of conduct

Their website can be found at: www.sra.org.uk. It has issued a code of conduct, which regulates the conduct of solicitors and their employees, solicitors who work in Europe, lawyers from abroad who work here, and other organisations and their employees. Consequently, if a paralegal works for a firm of solicitors or an organisation regulated by the Solicitors Regulation Authority, and that paralegal is the subject of a complaint, then the code of conduct will apply to them.

13.5: The ten principles of the code of conduct

The code describes itself as 'outcomes-focused' regulation. This means that rather than expecting an uninspired adherence to the rules, the code looks at the outcome that the solicitor should be trying to achieve. There are ten principles by which solicitors should abide. They should:

1. Uphold the rule of law and the proper administration of justice.
2. Act with integrity.

3. Not allow their independence to be compromised.
4. Act in the best interests of each client.
5. Provide a proper standard of service to their clients.
6. Behave in a way that maintains the trust the public places in them and in the provision of legal services.
7. Comply with their legal and regulatory obligations and deal with their regulators and Ombudsmen in an open, timely and co-operative manner.
8. Run their business or carry out their role in the business effectively and in accordance with proper governance and sound financial and risk management principles.
9. Run their business or carry out their role in the business in a way that encourages equality of opportunity and respect for diversity.
10. Protect client money and assets.

Solicitors are expected to communicate regularly with their clients and avoid delays. A client should never feel out of their depth with their solicitor or frightened to ask them questions. It is possible to report a solicitors' firm to the Solicitors Regulation Authority, which publishes guidance on when and how to take that step: http://www.sra.org.uk/consumers/problems/report-solicitor.page#how-complain.

It is often mistakenly thought by clients that if they complain to their lawyer, they will prejudice or damage the case their lawyer is running. There are some circumstances in which a mistake made by a lawyer is so serious that they cannot carry on acting for a client. However, a lawyer cannot simply abandon a client, particularly one who is legally aided, because they have complained. They have to deal with the complaint and see if it can be resolved.

Some clients may wish to change their solicitor. This may be difficult where the case is legally aided. The best course is to try to resolve the issue with the solicitor and then escalate to a full complaint if the solicitor will not respond.

13.6: Making a complaint against a solicitors firm

The Solicitors Regulation Authority has published a short guide on making a complaint to a solicitor, which can be found at: http://www.sra.org.uk/consumers/problems/report-solicitor.page#how-complain. The Legal Ombudsman (see p.214) provides a sample letter of complaint.

Every solicitors' firm should explain its complaints procedure in the very first letter, which it sends to the client. This is known as a 'client care letter' and it sets out basic points, i.e. who is dealing with the case, who supervises the person dealing with the case, what the client wants to achieve, how the solicitor is going to be paid and how much those costs will be, details of the firm's insurance, and the firm's complaints procedure.

The code of conduct published by the Solicitors Regulation Authority says that a solicitors' firm must have a written complaints procedure, which:

- ensures that clients' complaints are dealt with promptly, fairly, openly, and effectively
- is brought to clients' attention at the outset of the matter
- is easy for clients to use and understand, allowing for complaints to be made by any reasonable means
- is responsive to the needs of individual clients, especially those who are vulnerable
- enables complaints to be dealt with promptly and fairly, with decisions based on a sufficient investigation of the circumstances
- provides for appropriate remedies
- does not involve any charges to clients for handling their complaints.

The procedure must be provided to the client on request and, in the event that a client makes a complaint, they must be provided with all necessary information concerning the handling of the complaint. It must also give details of the Legal Ombudsman and the time limits for contacting the Ombudsman.

Complaints procedures in solicitors' firms normally have a two-stage process. The first stage is normally to get in touch with the lawyer by phone, email or letter and set out the complainant's concerns in order to see if they can be resolved there and then. If the problem cannot be resolved, then the second stage is to make a formal complaint setting out the issues. That complaint is then put to someone senior within the firm, who may be described as a 'complaints partner'. That senior person will then investigate the matter and respond with their views about the situation.

Failure to operate a firm's complaints procedure is a very serious matter, which should be reported to the Solicitors Regulation Authority. If the complaint cannot be resolved, then the next step is to contact the Legal Ombudsman.

13.7: Professional errors made by solicitors and conflicts of interest

Sometimes solicitors or their employees make mistakes and the effect on the client and their case can be devastating. A common error is failing to issue proceedings prior to a limitation date, such as the three year time limit in a personal injury claim. Another error is failing to complete a step in legal proceedings by a time limit set down by a court or tribunal.

Many errors made by solicitors firms are perfectly capable of being repaired without any kind of loss or prejudice to the client. However, sometimes the mistake is so serious that the solicitors firm has to consider whether it should cease to act because it can no longer act in the client's best interests. For instance, it may be in the solicitor's interest – having made the initial mistake – to bring the case to a swift close, whereas it may have always been in the client's interest to keep it running for as long as possible.

The solicitors firm is required to inform a current client if it discovers any act or omission which could give rise to a professional negligence claim by the client against the firm. They are not normally required to admit that what has happened is entirely their fault; what is required is an explanation of the mistake, and the effect it has on the case.

Sometimes the error is not so serious that the client has to go to another solicitor, but instead the firm will tell the client that they have the option of seeking independent legal advice, i.e. they can find another solicitor if they so wish. In this kind of situation, it may be wise to keep with the same firm, particularly if the mistake is capable of repair or, quite simply, it has not caused any real loss.

However, it may well be that a client is told that they have to go to a new firm. They will need to consider whether they have a professional negligence claim against their old firm. A specialist firm of solicitors will be required to handle such a claim.

Conflicts of interest can arise in other ways. A solicitor cannot normally act for a client who is making a claim against someone who is already the solicitor's client. A conflict can also arise where a solicitor is acting for two siblings, each of whom wants different things.

A solicitor has to be very careful if they are acting for a vulnerable person (for example, a child or a person without mental capacity in that matter) and the person representing that vulnerable person is clearly unsuitable.

Solicitors, of course, have to keep their client's details confidential. They are subject to the Data Protection Act (1998).

13.8: The Legal Ombudsman

The Legal Ombudsman was set up by S114 onwards of the Legal Services Act (2007). It covers: solicitors, barristers, licensed conveyancers, cost lawyers, legal executives, notaries, patent attorneys, and trade mark attorneys. They also cover claims management companies who handle accident management services and personal injury claims or mis-sold investment for pensions, as well as claims against banks for mis-selling insurance policies.

If the complaint cannot be resolved by the legal person or organisation, then the next step is to contact the Legal Ombudsman, which operates under its own scheme. Their website can be found at: www.legalombudsman.org.uk. The Legal Ombudsman's Scheme sets out the way in which they handle complaints and is recommended reading for anyone who is thinking of approaching the Ombudsman: www.legalombudsman.org.uk/helping-the-public/#scheme-rules.

As with other Ombudsmen, ordinarily a complainant cannot use the Legal Ombudsman unless the complainant has first gone through the complaints procedure available from the relevant legal person or organisation. There is a time limit. The complaint must be made to the Legal Ombudsman within six years from the act/omission of the solicitor or three years from when the complainant should reasonably have known there was cause for complaint. These time limits can be extended in certain circumstances.

A complainant can use the Legal Ombudsman if:

- the complaint has not been resolved to the complainant's satisfaction within eight weeks of being made to the 'authorised person' (legal person/organisation against whom the complaint was originally made); or
- an Ombudsman considers that there are exceptional reasons to consider the complaint sooner, or without it having been made first to the authorised person; or
- where an Ombudsman considers that in-house resolution is not possible due to irretrievable breakdown in the relationship between an authorised person and the person making the complaint.

If the Legal Ombudsman considers that there are exceptional circumstances, he/she may extend any of these time limits to the extent that he/she considers fair.

The Legal Ombudsman can decide not to consider a complaint, for instance where it feels that the complaint should best be handled by a court (this may be the case for a professional negligence claim).

The Legal Ombudsman can ask the relevant legal person/organisation to:

- apologise
- pay compensation of a specified amount for loss suffered
- pay interest on that compensation from a specified time
- pay compensation of a specified amount for inconvenience/distress caused
- ensure (and pay for) putting right any specified error, omission or other deficiency
- take (and pay for) any specified action in the interests of the complainant
- pay a specified amount for costs the complainant incurred in pursuing the complaint
- limit legal fees to a specified amount.

A binding and final determination can also be enforced through the courts by the Legal Ombudsman. The Ombudsman also publishes case summaries, grouped into categories of law, which can be found at: www.legalombudsman.org.uk/raising-standards/data-and-decisions/page/2/.

13.9: Key points

- Solicitors are heavily regulated and they are expected to operate effective complaints procedures as well as abide by a code of conduct laid down by their professional body, the Solicitors Regulation Authority.
- There are different types of lawyers – solicitors, barristers, chartered legal executives, paralegals and others who have their own regulatory bodies.
- Legal aid is very limited and many cases are simply too small to engage a lawyer – this is where complaints systems come in.
- Solicitors are bound by ten principles in the code of conduct.
- Every solicitors firm should explain its complaints procedure in the very first letter that it sends to the client. Complaints procedures in solicitors firms normally have a two-stage process.
- Watch out for professional errors and conflicts of interest.
- The Legal Ombudsman covers solicitors, barristers and other types of lawyers.

NO DISCRIMINATION · NO NEGLECT · NO ABUSE
DUTY OF CARE
PRISON ACT 1952
PRISON RULES 1999
FAIR TREATMENT IN PRISONS...

Chapter 14: Complaints about the prison and probation service

14.1: Introduction

The UK implemented the European Convention on Human Rights into law by enacting the Human Rights Act (1998). Article 3 of the convention provides that everyone should be free from oppression or torture. Prisoners and other kinds of detainees are particularly vulnerable to abuse and so the state is required to protect them by ensuring that there is an independent investigation of allegations of torture and inhumane or degrading treatment or punishment. The complaints system, which leads all the way up to the Prisons and Probation Ombudsman, is part of that process.

At the same time, deaths in custody are all too common. Article 2 of the convention provides that everyone has a 'right to life'. Furthermore, it says that there should be an independent and effective investigation into all deaths caused by the state (through use of force or failure to protect life). Any such investigation should be reasonably prompt, open to public scrutiny, and involve the next of kin of the deceased.

14.2: Different types of prisons

- Most adult prisoners are housed in various prisons up and down the country, which are categorised according to the risk that their prisoners present to the general public.
- Young offender institutions are prisons for 15 to 21 year olds.
- Secure training centres are for people aged up to 17. They provide education and training and follow a school day timetable.
- Secure children's homes or secure accommodation are run by local authorities. They are for children aged 10 to 14 years old. They also provide education and training and they follow a school day timetable.

14.3: Probation

Probation means that a person is still serving out their sentence but they are not in prison. A person who is a serving a community sentence, or who has been released from prison on licence or on parole, will generally be put on probation. Whilst on probation, that person may have to do unpaid work, complete an education or training course, get treatment for addictions and have regular meetings with an offender manager.

14.4: Her Majesty's Prison and Probation Service (HMPPS)

HMPPS is responsible for running prison and probation services. Their functions include rehabilitation services for people leaving prison, managing private sector prisons, and providing services such as the prisoner escort service and electronic tagging. They also oversee the custody of children and young people in secure training centres, young offender institutions, and secure accommodation.

14.5: The complaints system for prisoners

The management of prisons and the treatment of most adult prisoners are subject to the Prison Rules (1999), which are made by the government under S57 of the Prison Act (1952). These regulations/rules provide for the training and treatment of prisoners. For example, regulation 3 states that the purpose of the training and treatment of convicted prisoners shall be to encourage and assist them to lead a good and useful life. Regulation 49 deals with the use of restraint on prisoners.

14.5.1: Prison governors and independent monitoring boards

Prison governors manage the security of prisons, remand centres, and young offenders' institutions. They are the higher operational managers in the prison system. They may be responsible for a particular 'wing' or section of a prison rather than the whole prison.

Under the Prison Act (1952), it is a requirement that every prison is monitored by an independent monitoring board. The board's members are appointed by the government from volunteer members of the community, in which the prison is situated. A member of the board has access, at any time, to every part of the prison and to every prisoner. They can also interview any prisoner out of the sight and hearing of officers.

14.5.2: Making a complaint

Regulation 11 of the Prison Rules (1999) says that a prisoner may make a request or complaint to their relevant governor or independent monitoring board. The governor of the prison shall consider that complaint as soon as possible. A written complaint is confidential.

Regulation 78(1) says that the independent monitoring board for a prison and any member of the board shall hear any complaint or request, which a prisoner wishes to make to them.

Regulation 8 of the Young Offender Institution Rules 2000 and Regulation 8 of the Secure Training Centre rules (1998) contains the same rights to make a complaint.

Children in secure accommodation would normally make a complaint, under the Children Act (1989) complaints system, to the local authority, which runs the unit (see Chapter 4).

14.5.3: The Prison Service Instruction 02/2012

The actual complaints procedure for all prisons, youth offender institutions and secure training centres are contained within a document entitled Prison Service Instruction (PSI) 02/2012, which is published by the National Offender Management Service (now Her Majesty's Prison and Probation Service). This can be found at: www.justice.gov.uk/.../psi-2012/psi-02-2012-prisoner-complaints.doc. It is recommended reading for anyone who is considering submitting a complaint on behalf of a prisoner. PSI 02/2012 sets out a two stage complaints process.

Complaint forms (which are prescribed under PSI 02/2012) must be made freely available to prisoners. Prisoners must be informed about the complaints procedures during the 'early days' of their time in custody. Complaints will normally be made in writing and processed on working days only, although prisons must have arrangements in place to enable urgent complaints to be considered on non-working days.

Prisons must have arrangements in place, which will allow a prisoner to make a formal complaint orally to a member of staff where the prisoner has difficulty doing so in writing. In such circumstances, the complaint must be recorded and the written answer must be explained to the prisoner in due course.

Complaints should normally be submitted within three months of the incident or circumstances which give rise to the complaint, or the date on which they became known to the prisoner. Prisoners must receive a response to their complaint within five working days of the complaint being logged.

If a prisoner is dissatisfied with the response to his or her complaint, they may resubmit the complaint using an appeal form, setting out the reasons why. An appeal should normally be made within seven calendar days of the prisoner having received the initial response, unless there are exceptional reasons why this would have been difficult or impossible. The appeal form should be submitted in the same way as the original complaint form. Prisoners must receive a response to their appeal within five working days of the appeal being logged.

Appeals must be answered by someone at a higher level in the management structure than the person who provided the response to the original complaint. The time limits can vary depending on the type of complaint made. Annex B to PSI 02/2012 sets out those time limits. If the prisoner is dissatisfied with the appeal process, they can approach the Prisons and Probation Ombudsman.

14.6: Probation Instructions 51/2014 – the complaints system for people on probation

The National Probation Service was established by the Criminal Justice and Court Services Act (2000). It supervises high-risk offenders released into the community. It works alongside Community Rehabilitation Companies that manage low and medium risk offenders.

The predecessor to the Her Majesty's Prison and Probation Service, the National Offender Management Service, has published a Probation Standard Complaints Procedure under reference PI 51/2014. This sets out the government's 'probation instructions' on the complaints system to be operated by the National Probation Service and Community Rehabilitation Companies.

Once again, this is recommended reading for anyone who is submitting a complaint about the delivery of probation services to the National Probation Service or a Community Rehabilitation Company. The scheme can be found at: www.justice.gov.uk/offenders/probation-instructions.

14.7: The Prisons and Probation Ombudsman (PPO)

The PPO's website can be found at: www.ppo.gov.uk. The PPO sets out its terms of reference at: www.ppo.gov.uk/about/vision-and-values/terms-of-reference. This is not a particularly long document and is recommended reading for anyone wishing to approach the PPO.

The PPO has two main duties:

- To investigate complaints made by prisoners, young people in detention (prisons and secure training centres), offenders under probation supervision, and immigration detainees.
- To investigate deaths of prisoners, young people in detention, approved premises' residents, and immigration detainees due to any cause, including any apparent suicides and natural causes.

The PPO will investigate fatal incidents in secure children's homes or secure accommodation but not complaints from children and young people in these types of homes. As we saw in Chapter 4, these kinds of complaints can be brought under the procedures laid down in the Children's Homes (England) Regulations (2015).

Before putting a complaint to the PPO, a complainant must first seek redress through appropriate use of the relevant prison, youth detention accommodation, probation, or Home Office complaints procedure.

Complainants submitting their case to the PPO must do so within three calendar months of receiving a substantive reply in the internal complaint procedure. The PPO will not normally accept complaints where there has been a delay of more than 12 months between the complainant becoming aware of the relevant facts and submitting their case to the PPO, unless the delay has been the fault of the relevant authority and the PPO considers that it is appropriate to do so. The PPO has discretion to investigate those complaints where it considers there to be good reason for the delay, or where it considers the issues raised to be of sufficient severity to make an exception to the usual timeframe.

Once it has accepted the complaint, the PPO will undertake an investigation.

Fatalities are investigated by the fatal incidents teams. The PPO has an extensive archive of fatal incident reports on their website as well as report on incidents in various prisons.

The PPO cannot investigate:

- the clinical judgement of medical professionals
- policy decisions taken by a Minister of State
- cases currently the subject of civil litigation or criminal proceedings
- conviction, sentence, immigration status, reasons for immigration detention or the length of such detentions
- decisions or recommendations of the judiciary, the police, the Crown Prosecution Service and the Parole Board.

Many prisoners suffer from medical problems and there are often questions as to the standard of their medical care. Whilst the PPO cannot investigate a medical decision, their investigation can include examining the clinical issues relevant to each death. In the case of deaths in prisons, youth detention accommodation, secure children's homes, and immigration facilities, the PPO will ask NHS England to review the clinical care and examine the question of whether referrals to secondary healthcare were made appropriately.

A complainant who is dissatisfied with the way the PPO has dealt with his or her case can write a letter to request a review. The investigation will be reviewed by a member of senior staff who has not been involved in the case before. If there is some dispute about the failure to adequately investigate and the PPO closes their file, then the complainant is able to request that their MP refer the case to the Parliamentary and Health Service Ombudsman. For more information about the PHSO see Chapter 6 and their website www.ombudsman.org.uk.

14.8: Key points

- The UK implemented the European Convention on Human Rights into law by enacting the Human Rights Act (1998). Article 2 (the right to life) and Article 3 (the right to freedom from oppression and torture) are key rights for prisoners.
- There are different types of prisons – prisons for adults, young offender institutions, secure training centres and secure children's homes.
- A person on probation is still serving out their sentence but they are not in prison.
- The prison system is run by Her Majesty's Prison and Probation Service.

- The actual complaints procedure for all prisons, youth offender institutions, and secure training centres are contained within a document entitled Prison Service Instruction (PSI) 02/2012, which is published by the National Offender Management Service (now Her Majesty's Prison and Probation Service).

- There is a Probation Standard Complaints Procedure PI 51/2014, which sets out the scheme to be operated by the National Probation Service and Community Rehabilitation Companies.

- The Prisons and Probation Ombudsman investigates complaints made by prisoners and deaths.

Index of statutes and statutory instruments

Table of statutes

Administration of Justice Act (1985) … 13.3
Adoption and Children Act (2002) … 1.7; **4.2**; 4.3
Apprenticeships, Skills, Children and Learning Act (2009) … 7.7
Care Act (2014) … 1.7; **5.3**
    S67 … **5.3**
Care Standards Act (2000) … 6.9
Children Act (1989) … 3.1; 3.8.2; **4.1**; 4.2; 4.3; 4.4.7; 4.6; 5.2; 14.5.2
    S24D … **4.2**; **4.4.7**
    S24D(1) … **4.2**
    S25 … 4.6
    S26 – 3.1; **4.2**
    S26(3) … **4.2**
Children (Leaving Care) Act (2000) … **4.1**
Chronically Sick and Disabled Persons Act (1970) … 5.2
Consumer Rights Act (2015) … **11.5.1**
Consumers, Estate Agents and Redress Act (2007) … 11.8
    S42-52 … 11.8
Criminal Justice and Court Services Act (2000) … **14.6**
Data Protection Act (1998) … **1.9.3**; **2.7**; **12.2-12.6**; 13.7
    S7 … **2.7**; **12.5**
    S13 … **12.6**
    Schedule 1 … **12.4**
Domestic Violence, Crime and Victims Act (2004) … **10.13**; **10.18**
    S32 … **10.13**
    S48 … **10.18**
Education Act (1996) … **7.3.4**
    S342 … 7.5
    S496, S497 … **7.3.4**
Education Act (2002) … **7.3**
    S29 … **7.3**

In the following indexes, the chapter and paragraph numbers are in bold when the subject of that reference is discussed directly and is more than just a passing reference.

Equality Act (2010) ... **1.6.6**; 7.3.3
Freedom of Information Act (2000) ... 5.4.4; 6.6.3; **12.7**
Health and Social Care Act (2008) ... 5.4.6; **6.1**
    Part 1 ... 5.4.6
Health and Social Care (Community Health and Standards) Act (2003) ... **5.2**; **6.4**
    S113 ... **6.4**
    S114 ... **5.2**; 6.4
    S114(1)(b), S114(1)(c) ... **5.2**
    S115, S118, S119 ... **6.4**
Health and Social Care Act (2012) ... **6.3.1**; **6.3.2**; **6.8**
    S227(8) ... **6.8**
Health Commissioners Act (1993) ... **6.11**
    S8(1), S9(2), S9(3), S9(4), S10 ... **6.11**
    S18ZA, S18A ... **6.11**
Higher Education Act (2004) ... **7.6**
    S15 ... **7.6**
    Part 2 ... **7.6**
Schedule 1-4 ... 7.6
Housing Act (1996) ... **8.1**
    S51 ... **8.1**
    Schedule 2 ... **8.1**
Housing and Regeneration Act (2008) ... **8.6**
    S237 ... **8.6**
Human Rights Act (1998) ... 2.4.2; **14.1**
Immigration and Asylum Act (1999) ... 13.2
    S84 ... 13.2
Legal Services Act (2007) ... 13.1; 13.2; 13.3; **13.8**
    S14-S17 ... 13.2
    S114 ... **13.8**
Local Government Act (1974) ... **3.6.1-3.6.5**; **4.4.7**; **4.5**
    S25, S26 ... **3.6.1**
    S26A ... **4.4.7**
    S27(1) ... **3.6.2**
    S26(4) ... **3.6.4**
    S26(6) ... **3.6.3**
    S26(12) ... **3.6.4**
    S28, S29, S30, S30(3), S30(4), S30(4A), S30(5), S31, S31A ... **3.6.5**
    S59(4)(b) ... **4.5**
    Part III ... **3.6.1**
    Schedule 5 ... **3.6.3**

Local Government Act (2000) ... **3.3**
    S92 ... **3.3**
Localism Act (2011) ... **8.3**
    S180 ... **8.3**
Mental Capacity Act (2005) ... 1.2; 5.3; **6.10.1**
    S35(1) ... **6.10.1**
Mental Health Act (1983) ... 1.2; **6.10.2**
    S130A ... **6.10.2**
Police Reform Act (2002) – 10.1; 10.3; **10.5**; **10.8**
    S12 ... **10.5**; **10.8**;
Schedule 3 ... 10.3
Police Reform and Social Responsibility Act (2011) ... **10.1**
Policing and Crime Act (2017) ... **10.1**; **10.3**; **10.19**
Postal Services Act (2011) ... 11.2
    S51 ... 11.2
Prison Act (1952) ... **14.5**
    S57 ... 14.5
Public Service Ombudsman Bill (Draft) ... **3.7**; **6.11**; **8.7**; 10.14
    S26 ... **3.7**; **8.7**
Solicitors Act (1974) ... 13.2; 13.3
    S21 ... 13.2
Telecommunications Act (1984) ... 11.2
    S27E ... 11.2
Water Industry Act (1991) ... 11.2
    S38, S39, S95, S96 ... 11.2

Table of statutory instruments

Adoption Agency Regulations (1976) ... 12.4
Adoption Agency Regulations (1983) ... 12.4
Adoption Agencies Regulations (2005) ... 12.4
Advocacy Services and Representations Procedure (Children) (Amendment) Regulations (2004) ... **4.3**
    Reg. 3, 4, 5 ... **4.3**
Alternative Dispute Resolution for Consumer Disputes (Competent Authorities and Information) Regulations (2015) ... **11.5.3**
    Reg. 19 ... 11.5.3
Arrangement for Placement of Children Regulations (1991) ... 12.4
Arrangements for Placement of Children by Voluntary Organisations and Others (England) Regulations (2011) ... 12.4

Index of statutes and statutory instruments

Care and Support (Independent Advocacy Support) (No 2) Regulations (2014) … **5.3**
    Reg. 2, 5, 6 … **5.3**
Care Planning, Placement and Case Review (England) Regulations (2010) … 12.4
Children Act 1989 Representations Procedure (England) Regulations (2006) … 3.1; **4.4-4.5**
    Reg. 5, 6, 8 … **4.4.3**
    Reg. 9 … 3.1; **4.4**
    Reg. 10 … **4.4.6**
    Reg. 11 … **4.4.7**
    Reg. 12 … **4.4.8**
    Reg. 13 … 4.5
    Reg. 14 … **4.4.9**; 4.4.10
    Reg. 15, 16 … **4.4.9**
    Reg. 17 … **4.4.9**; **4.4.10**
    Reg. 18 … **4.4.10**; **4.4.11**
    Reg. 19 … **4.4.11**
    Reg. 21, 22 … **4.5**
    Reg. 22(2)(b) … 4.5
Children's Homes (England) Regulations (2015) … **4.6**; 14.7
    Reg 39 – **4.6**
The Data Protection (Subject Access Modification) (Education) Order (2000) … 12.5

The Data Protection (Subject Access Modification) (Health) Order (2000) …12.5

The Data Protection (Subject Access Modification) (Social Work) Order (2000) … 12.5

Education (Independent School Standards) Regulations (2014) … **7.4**
    Part 7 of the Schedule … **7.4**
Education (Investigation of Parents' Complaints) (England) Regulations (2007) … **7.3.5**
The Fostering Services (England) Regulations (2011) … **4.7**
    Reg. 18 … **4.7**
Gas and Electricity (Consumer Complaints Handling Standards) Regulations (2008) … **11.8**
    Reg. 8 … **11.8**
Health and Social Care Act (2008) (Regulated Activities) Regulations (2014) … **6.1**
    Reg. 20 … **6.1**;
    Part 4 … **6.1**

Local Authority Social Services and National Health Service Complaints Regulations (2009) … 5.2; **5.4-5.5**; **6.6-6.6.6**
- Reg. 3 … **6.6.1**
- Reg. 3(2) … **5.4.1**
- Reg. 4 … **5.4.2**; **6.6.2**
- Reg. 5, 5(2), 5(3), 5(4), 5(5) … **5.4.3**
- Reg. 8 … **5.4.4**; **6.6.3**
- Reg. 9 … **5.4.5**; **6.6.4**
- Reg. 11 … **5.4.6**; **6.6.4**
- Reg. 11(3) … **5.4.6**
- Reg. 12 … **5.4.7**; **6.6.5**
- Reg. 13 … **5.4.8**; **6.6.5**
- Reg. 14 … **5.4.8**; **6.6.6**;
- Reg. 14(4) … **5.4.9**;
- Reg. 15 … **6.6.6**
- Reg. 16 … **5.5**; **6.6.6**
- Reg. 17, 18 … **6.6.6**

Mental Capacity Act (2005) (Independent Mental Capacity Advocates) (General) Regulations (2006) …**6.10.1**

Mental Capacity Act (2005) (Independent Mental Capacity Advocates) (Expansion of Role) Regulations (2006) …**6.10.1**
- Reg. 4 … **6.10.1**

Mental Health Act 1983 (Independent Mental Health Advocates) (England) Regulations (2008) … **6.10.2**
- Reg. 6 … **6.10.2**

NHS Bodies and Local Authorities (Partnership Arrangements, Care Trusts, Public Health and Local Healthwatch) Regulations (2012) … **6.7**
- Reg. 20-33 … **6.7**

Part 5 … **6.7**

Non-maintained Special Schools (England) Regulations (2015) … **7.5**

Police (Complaints and Misconduct) Regulations (2012) … **10.3**; **10.11**

Prison Rules (1999) … **14.5**; **14.5.2**; **14.5**
- Reg. 3 … **14.5**
- Reg. 11 … **14.5.2**
- Reg. 45 … **14.5**
- Reg. 78(1) … **14.5.2**

Private and Voluntary Healthcare (England) Regulations (2001) … **6.9**
- Reg. 23 … **6.9**

Secure Training Centre Rules (1998) … **14.5.2**
- Reg. 8 … **14.5.2**

Water Supply and Sewerage Services (Customer Service Standards) Regulations (2008) … **11.8**

Reg. 8 ... **11.8**
Young Offender Institution Rules (2000) ... **14.5.2**
Reg. 8 ... **14.5.2**

Table of European legislation

EU Directive 2013/11/EU – **11.5.3**

Table of international legislation

European Convention on Human Rights ... 2.4.2; 10.9.5; **14.1**
Articles 2, 3 ... 2.4.2; **14.1**
Articles 4,5,6,8, 14 ... 2.4.2
Protocol 1 Art 2 ... 2.4.2;

Table of guidance

Best Practice Advice for School Complaints Procedures (2016) ... **7.3.1**
Care and Support Statutory Guidance (2017) ... **5.3**
Getting the Best from Complaints (2006) ... **4.4.1**
Guidance on Good Practice: Remedies (2017) ... **3.6.6**
Investigation Manual for the Local Government and Social Care Ombudsman (2016) ... **3.6.7**
National Standards for the Provision of Children's Advocacy Services (2002) ... **1.8**
No Secrets: Guidance on Developing and Implementing Multi-Agency Policies and Procedures to Protect Vulnerable Adults from Abuse ... **6.10.1**
Prison Service Instruction 02/(2012) ... **14.5.3**
Probation Instructions 51/(2014) ... **14.6**
Statutory guidance to the police service on the handling of complaints ... **10.3**; 10.11

Subject index

Access to advocacy ... **1.7**
Access to justice ... 1.11
Act of Parliament ... **3.1**
Adoption ... **4.2**
Adult social services ... Chapter 5
Advocacy charter, the ... **1.8**
Advocacy process, the ... **2.4**; 2.6
Advocacy Quality Performance Mark, the ... **1.8**
Advocacy referral ... **2.2**
Advocacy training ... **1.5**; **1.6-1.6.7**; **1.8**; **1.9-1.9.5**
Alternative Dispute Resolution (ADR) ... 7.6; **11.5.2- 11.5.4**
Antisocial behaviour ... 8.4
Balance of probabilities ... 2.8
Bar Council and Bar Standards Board ... **13.1**; 13.2
Benefits – Chapter 9, see also ... **3.8.3**
British Association for Counselling and Psychotherapy ... 6.8
Care Act Advocate (CAA) ... 1.2; 1.7; **5.3**
Care Quality Commission, the ... 3.8.4; **6.1**; 6.3.1
Care Standards ... **3.8.4**
Care leaver ... **4.1**; **4.2**; 4.4.7
Casework Division Head ... **10.14**
Chief Crown Prosecutor ... **10.14**
Child Maintenance Service ... 9.1
Child in need ... **4.1**; 5.2;
Child Sexual Abuse Review Panel ... 10.17
Children Act proceedings ... see **3.8.2**
Children's homes ... **4.5**; **4.6**
Children's social services – Chapter 4
Citizens Advice Bureaux (CAB) ... **11.2**
Client care letter ... 13.6
Clinical Commissioning Group (CCG) ... **6.3.1**
Clinical negligence ... **6.5**
Conflict of interest ... **13.7**
Communication
    Alternative/augmented methods of communication ... 1.3; **1.4**; 2.3;
    Dealing with hostility ... 2.6.3; **2.6.4**
    Communication with clients ... **1.3**; **1.4**; **1.6.2**; 2.3; **2.4.1-4**; 2.6.3;
    Communication with professionals ... **2.5.1**; **2.6.2-3**

Compensation ... **2.4.2**; **3.3**; 3.6.6; 3.8; 3.8.1; **3.8.7**; 5.4.4; 5.4.8; 8.6; 10.1; 10.3; 11.8; 12.6.1; 13.8;
        Personal injury claims ... **3.8.7**
        Criminal Injuries Compensation Authority (CICA) ... **3.8.8**
Consumer Council for Water ... **11.4**
Complaint forms ... **2.5.1**
Confidentiality ... 1.9; **1.9.2**
Consent form ... 2.3; 2.5.2; 2.7;
Criminal Injuries Compensation Authority (CICA) ... see **compensation**
Crown Prosecution Service ... Chapter 10
Data controller ... **12.3**
Data processor ... **12.3**
Data Protection ... Chapter 12
see also ... 1.9; **1.9.3**; 2.5.1; 2.6.1; 2.7
Data subject ... **12.3**
Death and Serious Injury (DSI) matters ... **10.8**
Department for Education ... 3.5; 7.1; 7.3; 7.3.1; 7.3.2; 7.3.4; 7.4; 7.5
Department for Work and Pensions (DWP) ... 9.1; 9.3
Designated person ... **8.3**; 8.4; 8.5
Designated tenant panel ... **8.3**
Direction and control matters... **10.8**
Disapplication ... 10.7; **10.9.2**
Discontinuance ... **10.10**
Discrimination ... **1.6.6**; 10.4
Dispute resolution ... see **Alternative Dispute Resolution**
Duty to cooperate ... **3.2**; 5.1; **5.4.5**; **6.6.4**
Duty of candour ... **6.1**
Duty to provide information ... **10.9.9**
Education and Skills Funding Agency ... 7.4; 7.7
Education ... Chapter 7
Form of authority ... see **consent form**
Foster care ... **4.7**
Freedom of Information ... **12.7**
General Chiropractic Council ... 6.8
General Dental Council ... 6.8
General Medical Council ... 6.8
General Optical Council ... 6.8
General Osteopathic Council ... 6.8
General Pharmaceutical Council ... 6.8
Healthcare including mental health... Chapter 6
Health and Care Professions Council ... **6.8**
Health and Wellbeing Board ... **6.3.1**

Subject index

Healthwatch England ... **6.3.1**
Her Majesty's Prison and Probation Service (HMPPS) ... **14.4**
Homes and Communities Agency ... 8.6
Housing and planning issues ... Chapter 8
Human rights ... 2.4.2; **14.1**
Independent Assessor of Complaints ... 3.5; **10.14**
Independent Case Examiner ... 9.3
Independent Domestic Violence Advocate (IDVA) ... 1.2; 1.5; 10.13
Independent Healthcare Advisory Services ... **6.9**
Independent Mental Capacity Advocate (IMCA) ...1.2; 1.5; 5.3; **6.10.1**
Independent Mental Health Advocates (IMHA) ... 1.2; 1.5; **6.10.2**
Independent Monitoring Board ... **14.5.1**
Independent Office for Police Conduct (IOPC) ... **3.1**; **3,2**; **3.5**; **10.1**; **10.2**; **10.3**; 10.5; 10.9.3; 10.94; **10.9.7**; **10.9.8**; **10.10**; **10.11**; **10.19**
Independent Person (children's social services) ... **4.4.10**; **4.4.11**
Independent Police Complaints Commission (IPCC) ... **10.1**; **10.2**
Independent Schools Inspectorate ... **7.4**
Independent Sector Complaints Adjudication Service (ISCAS) ... 6.9
Independent Sexual Violence Advocate (ISVA) ... 1.2; 1.5; 10.13
Information Commissioner's Office (ICO) ... 2.7; 3.5; 6.11; **12.2**; **12.6.2**; 12.7
Initial agreement form ... **2.3**
Initial meeting with client ... **2.3**
Investigating officer (children's social services) ... **4.4.10**; **4.4.11**
Investigating officer (police) ... **10.9.6**
Judicial review ... 2.9; 3.8; **3.8.1**; 3.8.2
Letter of claim/letter before claim ... **3.8.1**; 3.8.7;
Law Society, the ... 13.1; 13.2; 13.3
Lawyers, types of ... 13.1
Legal Services Board ... **13.1**
Legal aid ... 3.8; 3.8.1; 13.2; 13.3
Legal routes ... 3.8-3.8.8
Lone working ... **1.9.4**; 2.3
Maladministration ... **3.3**
Mental capacity ... 1.3; 5.4.3; 6.10.1
Mental health ... Chapter 6
    see also ... **3.8.5**
National Health Service (NHS)... see **healthcare**
National Standards for Advocacy ... **1.8**
Neighbour nuisance ... 8.4
NHS England/ NHS Commissioning Board – **6.3.1**
NHS trusts – **6.3.1**
'No win no fee' ... 3.8.8;

Non-instructed advocacy … **1.3**
Nursing and Midwifery Council … 6.8
Office of Communications (Ofcom) … **11.2**
Office of Gas and Electricity Markets (Ofgem) … **11.2**
Office of the Independent Adjudicator … **7.6**
Ofsted … 3.8.4; 4.6; 4.7; **7.3.5**; 7.7
Ombudsman … **3.5**
  Housing Ombudsman … 3.5; 3.7; 8.1; 8.2; 8.3; 8.4; **8.5**
  Legal Ombudsman … 3.5; 13.1; 13.6; **13.8**
  Local Government and Social Care Ombudsman (LGSCO) … 3.5; **3.6-3.6.7**; 3.7; **4.8**; 5.4.5; 5.4.8; 5.5; 6.6.6; 8.2; 8.7; 8.8; 9.1; 12.6.2
  Ombudsman Association … **3.5**; 7.6
  Ombudsmen Services … 3.5; **11.4**; **11.5.4**
  Parliamentary and Health Service Ombudsman (PHSO) … 3.3; 3.5; 3.7; 6.4; 6.6.6; 6.9; **6.11**; 8.7; 8.8; 9.1; 9.4; 10.14
  Prisons and Probation Ombudsman … 3.5; 6.11; 14.1; **14.7**
  Public Service Ombudsman Bill (Draft) … **3.7**; **6.11**; **8.7**; 10.14
Patient Advice and Liaison Service (PALS) … **6.5**
Personal injury claims … see **compensation**
Planning Inspectorate … **8.8**
Police and Crown Prosecution Service … Chapter 10
Pre-action letter … see **letter of claim**
Prison and Probation … Chapter 14
Professional Standards Authority for Health and Social Care … 6.8
Public health … **6.3.2**
Records … see **subject access request**
Registered Intermediary … **10.15**
Regulation … **3.1**
Regulator of Social Housing … **8.6**
Remedies … **2.4.2-3**; **3.6.6**; 4.10; 5.7; 6.11
Risk assessments … **1.9.4**; 2.3; 2.6.4;
Safeguarding … 1.9; **1.9.1**
School Complaints Unit … **7.3.4**
School Inspection Service … **7.4**
Schools, types of … **7.2**; **7.3**
Secure children's homes … 4.6; 14.2; 14.5.2; 14.7
Secure training centres … 14.2; 14.5.2; 14.7
Social housing … **8.1**
Solicitors Regulation Authority … **13.1**; 13.2; **13.3**; **13.4**; 13.6
Special Educational Needs (SEN) … **3.8.6**; 7.1
Statute … see **Act of parliament**
Statutory instrument … see **Regulation**

Subject access request ... **2.7**; 12.2; **12.5**
Supervision ... **1.9.5**
Tenancy Standard ... 8.6
Tribunals ... **3.8**
    First-tier Tribunal (Social Security and Child Support) ... **3.8.3**
    First-tier Tribunal (Care Standards) ... **3.8.4**
    First-tier Tribunal (Mental Health) ... **3.8.5**; 6.10
    First-tier Tribunal (Special Educational Needs and Disability) ... **3.8.6**
Utilities and private companies ... Chapter 11
Victim of crime ... **10.13**; 10.14; 10.16; 10.17; 10.18
Victims' Commissioner ... **10.18**
Victim Personal Statement (VPS) ... **10.13**
Victims' Right to Review Scheme ... 10.13; 10.14; **10.16**
Water Industry Redress Scheme ... **11.4**
Water Services Regulation Authority (Ofwat) ... **11.2**
Witness Charter ... **10.15**
Young offender institutions ... 14.2; 14.5.2; 14.7